JANE E
A WORKSHEI

CW00422442

Jane O'N _
Formerly Head of English
Long Road Sixth Form College
Cambridge

**Literary Images
Limited**

First published in the UK in 1996 by
Literary Images Limited
11 Wardour Mews
London W1V 3FF

© Jane O'Neill 1996
ISBN 1 874274 04 5

Printed in Great Britain by Robendene

Contents

Introduction

This 'study guide' to *Jane Eyre* aims at drawing attention to the main elements or aspects of the novel which any serious reader must address, e.g. the main 'themes', imagery - in which *Jane Eyre* is so rich - the role of narrator, structure and style. The Guide is not intended to present a particular critical viewpoint of *Jane Eyre*, for which the reader should turn to the many critical studies available.

By asking very specific questions and demanding close textual reference in support of answers, the Student Worksheet directs the reader to look closely at the text. The Worksheet Guide provides suggested interpretations, where appropriate or necessary, and specific textual reference for the questions asked on the student sheet (to enable readers to find these references and quotations easily, page numbers to both the Penguin Classics editions of the novel are given - the 1985 edition in parentheses; the 1996 edition in square brackets).

Readers should note that where there is any discrepancy in the text quoted from that found in the Penguin edition, the quotation is taken from The World's Classics edition, edited by Margaret Smith. It is based on "the first edition of *Jane Eyre* (Smith, Elder 1847), which has been collated throughout with the MS and with the second and third editions", while the Penguin Classics edition is the third edition, as the notes on page 479 (1985 edition) explain. Such discrepancies between the texts are to be found in punctuation and spelling and, occasionally, in phrasing and vocabulary. (For instance, "...a bright beck, full of dark stones and sparkling *edges*" on page 107 in the 1985 Penguin edition is "...a bright beck, full of dark stones and sparkling *eddies*" on page 76 in the World's Classics edition). These discrepancies should not cause any problems for the reader.

Teachers should find this Guide useful in preparing the text for teaching, in actually working through the novel with a class, and in revision. Students themselves find it a very useful self-help tool, both in studying the novel and in revising for examinations. Space has been left at the end of each section for the reader's own notes. The author has used these textually-based worksheets very successfully with A level students for a number of years.

Although this 'study guide' should prove helpful to both students and teachers, it is not intended only for them. The detailed Guide, providing specific textual references, should be useful to all those who want help with approaching a text in greater critical depth.

Jane O'Neill

THE SIGNIFICANCE OF PLACE (Q.1).

Anyone who has read *Jane Eyre* has formed a very definite picture in his or her mind of the places described in the novel, particularly of Lowood and Thornfield. Barbara Hardy sees the novel as concerned with, among other things, Jane's search for home, and it is certainly useful to look at *Jane Eyre* and the places where she lives in the light of this.

Gateshead: A place of alienation, where Jane is an outcast in the family - emphasised by all the weather images of cold and rain and wind, and by the images of cruelty and imprisonment which characterize the opening pages of the novel. She is an orphan, isolated and friendless, "less than a servant" in the words of the lady's-maid (**p.44**) [**19**]. "I was a discord in Gateshead Hall" she says of herself (**p.47**) [**23**]. The rain beats and the wind howls and "I grew by degrees cold as a stone" she tells us on **page 48** [**23**]. Her sense of imprisonment is reflected particularly, of course, in the incident of the red-room, but also in such phases as "'you are like a slave-driver", (**p.43**) [**17**] spoken to John Reed - who bullies her incessantly with his mother's blessing - "like any other rebel slave" (**p.44**) [**19**], in her reference to "bonds" (**p.44**) [**19**], and even in her waking image of the nursery fire "crossed with thick black bars" (**p.51**) [**26**], reminiscent of a prison window. Charlotte Brontë gives us no general description of Gateshead; we experience it through Jane's experience. For her it is in no sense a home, but a place from which she must escape if she is to develop into the independent and integrated self which she becomes by the end of the novel.

Lowood: Our first impressions of Lowood suggest that Jane has left Gateshead for an environment at least as bad if not worse. We are given much more detailed description of the school than of Gateshead. "I passed from compartment to compartment, from passage to passage, of a large and irregular building; till... we came upon the hum of many voices, and presently entered a wide long room, with great deal tables, two at each end, on each of which burnt a pair of candles, and seated all round on benches, a congregation of girls of every age from nine or ten to twenty", Jane tells us on **page 76** [**53**]. Except for her description of the red-room Charlotte Brontë gives us no such physical sense of place at Gateshead.

At Lowood injustice, punishment, sadism are rife, as well as physical deprivation - cold and hunger. But there are redeeming aspects of her life here: her friendship with Helen Burns, her love and respect for Miss Temple and Miss Temple's genuine concern for and dedication to the welfare of her pupils; and, just as important as these, the opportunity which Lowood affords her to pursue her education and, therefore, the development of her mind and character. The link between these and her longing for independence will be explored in later questions. By the time Jane leaves Lowood she has experienced many redeeming human qualities: friendship, love, unselfishness; she has learnt, also, through the example of Helen Burns, to curb somewhat the unrestrained passion which characterizes her at Gateshead. Lowood could never have been more than a temporary home for Jane , but at it she has experienced qualities which she had only hints of at Gateshead in the erratic moments of affection shown her by Bessie.

Thornfield: Here, of course, Jane finds love, but note the name of the house - it is a place of thorns. Her dreams of happiness and fulfilment are dashed just as the chestnut-tree in the garden is struck by lightning. What had seemed to her like her permanent home becomes, when she learns the truth about Rochester's status, as much of a prison as it is for mad Bertha in the attic. Here, though, is the place where reason and principle triumph over passion: Jane's Christian faith and moral strength enable her, at tremendous cost, to withstand Rochester's pleading with her to live with him as his mistress, and she becomes homeless once again. We might have suspected, if we had thought about it, that this battlemented house, reminiscent of a fortress, would turn out to be another place of confinement for Jane; she does not find here the freedom she seeks, because the man she loves is not legally or morally free to consummate that love.

Moor House: This is another temporary home for Jane, a "port in a storm". She is drawn to it first by the light in its window, beckoning her in the darkness, "The light was yet there; shining dim, but constant, through the rain" (**p.357**) [**371**]. And as she comes to the house she looks through the kitchen window and describes the homely and cheerful scene within. The passage is marked by images of light: "radiance", "glowing", "peat-fire", "candle", "rays", "beacon", "light" (**p.358**) [**372**], which suggest that this is a place where she will be welcome and where she will be happy, so far as this is possible for her, separated from Rochester. It is, of course, the place where she discovers that she is not so isolated and friendless as she has always believed and felt herself to be. The people of Moor House are her cousins - for the first time in her life she has a family. It is here, too, that she rejects St John's offer of marriage, because she does not love him and because she cannot deny the passion in her own nature. This passion she shares with Rochester, symbolised by the call from him which she hears and obeys (**pp.444 ff.**) [**466 ff.**]. We have a strong physical sense of Moor House (also called Marsh End, see **p.368** [**382**]), with its "gray, small antique structure, with its low roof, its latticed casements, its mouldering walls, its avenue of aged firs - all grown aslant under the stress of mountain winds; its garden, dark with yew and holly..." (**p.376**) [**391**] and, on **page 379** [**394**], St

John's "window-recess - which his table, chair, and desk consecrated as a kind of study..." It is a homely house, which offers Jane a refuge, but it cannot be her permanent home because that can only be with Rochester.

Ferndean: When Jane approaches Ferndean (Chapter 37), she tells us that it is "deep buried in a wood", the evening is "marked by the characteristics of sad sky, cold gale, and continued small, penetrating rain." She cannot see the house for "the gloomy wood about it" and she finds herself "in the twilight of close-ranked trees"; "The darkness of natural as well as sylvan dusk gathered over me" (**p.455**) [**478**]. The images of darkness, rain, and, on **page 457** [**481**], the reference to "This parlour looked gloomy: a neglected handful of fire burnt low in the grate" all reflect Rochester's sadness and isolation. Symbolically, Jane takes from Mary, the servant, the glass of water which she was bringing Rochester; it is Jane who brings him the water of life that symbolises their love and future together.

The darkness of Ferndean is transformed by the light of their love and happiness. On **page 475** [**499**] Rochester tells Jane, "...our honey-moon will shine our life long: its beams will only fade over your grave or mine." And the light which Jane brings back into his life is symbolised also by the regaining of some of his sight, so that "he can find his way without being led by the hand: the sky is no longer a blank to him, the earth no longer a void. When his first-born was put into his arms, he could see that the boy had inherited his own eyes, as they once were - large, brilliant and black." (**p.476**) [**501**].

Ferndean, then, becomes Jane's true home, because here she is united with the man she loves. Her search for fulfilment, for independence is over: "To be together is for us to be at once as free as in solitude, as gay as in company...All my confidence is bestowed on him; all his confidence is devoted to me: we are precisely suited in character; perfect concord is the result." (**p.476**) [**500**].

Notes:

FREEDOM, INDEPENDENCE AND SERVITUDE (Q.2).

From the opening pages of the novel we are made aware of Jane's passionate desire for freedom. At Gateshead, a place of servitude, she sees John Reed as a "slave-driver" and herself as a "rebel slave". What she hopes to achieve by going to school is independence and freedom. She doesn't achieve it at Lowood, of course, but she does acquire there the education which enables her to pursue her search for it. When she is deciding to leave Lowood, she looks out on the hilly horizon and longs to surmount the "blue peaks", "all within their boundary of rock and heath seemed prison-ground, exile limits." (**p.117**) [**99**] and she goes on to say, "'I tired of the routine of eight years in one afternoon. I desired liberty; for liberty I gasped; for liberty I uttered a prayer; it seemed scattered on the wind then faintly blowing... I cried, half desperate, 'Grant me at least a new servitude!'" (**p.117**) [**99**].

By liberty Jane means the freedom to think and act for herself, to be her 'own mistress', as she calls herself to Rochester at the end of the novel (**p.459**) [**483**]. Her 'independence' is gained financially through the bequest from her uncle, but it is as much a state of mind and heart as it is financial.

It is interesting to note that it is in the pages dealing with St John's attempt to persuade her to marry him that most of the references to freedom and servitude are to be found. Marriage to St John would be servitude for Jane. He is himself in servitude to a rigid moral and religious code which prevents him from ackowledging the needs of his human nature. Jane describes him when Miss Oliver calls, "His chest heaved once, as if his large heart, weary of despotic constriction, had expanded, despite the will, and made a vigorous bound for the attainment of liberty. But he curbed it, I think, as a resolute rider would curb a rearing steed" (**pp.390,391**) [**407**].

As he curbs himelf, so does he Jane. On **page 423** [**443**] she tells us, "By degrees, he acquired a certain influence over me that took away my liberty of mind: his praise and notice were more restraining than his indifference." And on the following page she says when he kisses her goodnight, "I felt as if this kiss were a seal affixed to my fetters."

In contrast, when she returns to Rochester she feels no such constraints. He is like a "fettered wild beast or bird... The caged eagle, whose gold-ringed eyes cruelty has extinguished" (**p.456**) [**479**], but the fetters are not extended to her. In fact, she brings freedom as well as light to Rochester. As she says on **page 476** [**500**], "To be together is for us to be at once as free as in solitude..." Love freely given and received is liberating.

So Jane, by the end of the novel, has left her servitude behind. She has financial independence and her independence of mind and heart are nurtured rather than curbed by Rochester's love. His favourite images for her reinforce this. She is an "eager bird" (**p.337**) [**349**], his "linnet" (**p.339**) [**351**], his "sky-lark" (**p.464**) [**488**], his "mocking changeling - fairy-born and human-bred"(**p.463**) [**487**]. This is only one of the many references to Jane as a fairy creature, elusive and other-wordly, which Rochester uses in the novel. On **page 296** [**300**], for instance, he speaks of Jane to Adèle as "a fairy...come from Elf-land...and its errand was to make me happy." He allows her then, even cherishes, the independence which she seeks, so she is free to give him her love unchained and uncurbed without losing her independence.

OTHER SUGGESTED REFERENCES:

a)   Rochester says of Jane: "'Consider that eye: consider the resolute, wild, free thing looking out of it...Whatever I do with its cage, I cannot get at it...If I tear, if I rend the slight prison, my outrage will only let the captive loose.'" (**pp.344,345**) [**357**]. He is trying to persuade Jane to stay with him after she learns that he is already married; but she is resolute in her independent decision to leave him.

b)   When St John asks Jane to take over the little school at Morton, she says, "...compared with that of a governess in a rich house, it was independent; and the fear of servitude with strangers entered my soul like iron..." (**p.381**) [**397**].

c)   On **page 446** [**469**] Jane says of the call she has heard from Rochester, "...it had opened the doors of the soul's cell, and loosed its bands..."

Notes:

JUSTICE AND PUNISHMENT (Q.3).

"'Unjust! - unjust!' said my reason…'" are Jane's words after she has been "wantonly" struck by John Reed in Chapter 2 of the novel (**p.47**) [**22**]. And, when she is wanted by Mrs Reed in the breakfast-room, she says of herself, "What a miserable little poltroon had fear, engendered of unjust punishment, made of me in those days!" (**p.63**) [**40**].

But it is in her conversation with Helen Burns after Helen has been "flogged" by Miss Scatcherd that Jane makes clear her stand on the subject: "'If people were always kind and obedient to those who are cruel and unjust, the wicked people would have it all their own way'" and "'I must resist those who punish me unjustly'" (**p.90**) [**68**]. She is resisting Helen's Christian message of 'love your enemies, and bless those who persecute you', though "I suspected she might be right and I wrong" (**p.88**) [**66,67**]. Helen goes on to say that, with her belief in Eternity as a home for all, "'…injustice never crushes me too low: I live in calm, looking to the end'" (**p.91**) [**70**]. Helen's passive acceptance of suffering and punishment contrasts markedly with Jane's rebellion. When Helen is forced to wear a board with the word 'Slattern' on it, "regarding it as a deserved punishment", Jane "ran to Helen, tore it off, and thrust it into the fire: the fury of which she was incapable had been burning in my soul all day, and tears, hot and large, had continually been scalding my cheek; for the spectacle of her sad resignation gave me an intolerable pain at the heart" (**pp.105,106**) [**86**].

Jane's passionate sense of what is just and unjust is a dominating force in the early part of the novel. When Mr Brocklehurst denounces her in front of the school, she tells Miss Temple she can never cry her grief away "'Because I have been wrongly accused'", and when Miss Temple clears her name, Jane is "relieved of a grievous load". Although, by the end of the novel, she has learned to temper her passionate nature, her sense of justice is to be seen in the sharing of her inheritance with her cousins and in her even-handed appreciation of St John, who is in so many ways antipathetic to her. While she was not able to share his calling, she sees "his glorious sun hastens to its setting" and "his incorruptible crown" is his just reward. (**p.477**) [**502**].

Notes:

PASSION (Q.4).

Jane's passionate nature colours every part of her life. We see it throughout the novel from the first chapter when she shouts and flies at John Reed - "'Did anybody ever see such a picture of passion!'" (p.43) [18] - to the concluding pages when she recounts the passionate mystical exchange between her and Rochester (pp.471,472) [496,497].

We have already looked at her passionate belief in justice and resistance to unjust punishment, as experienced both at Gateshead and Lowood. We have seen how her passionate nature is contrasted with Helen Burns' rational, passive response to suffering and punishment.

During the course of the novel, Jane learns to control her passionate nature, her hardest test, of course, being the choice she makes to leave Rochester; but when she rejects St John's 'offer' of marriage and hears Rochester calling her, she is, of course, obeying the passionate core of her being, which responds to his. Rochester is the only other character in the novel who shares Jane's passionate nature, which is why they are "precisely suited in character" (p.476) [500]. By the end of the novel they have earned their reward - the enjoyment of that mutual passion - because they have learnt to control it, to subjugate it to morality and principle (Jane's decision to leave Thornfield, Rochester's risking of his life to save Bertha, the obstacle to his marriage to Jane).

Notes:

ISOLATION (Q.5).

There are several ways in which Charlotte Brontë makes us aware of the isolation of her characters. Jane, for instance, is isolated emotionally from the Reed family, and that sense of loneliness is reinforced by her physical isolation from them: behind the window curtain, alone in the nursery, etc. Repeatedly, we are told of her being alone: "I enjoyed my conqueror's solitude" (**p.69**) [**46**], she comments after she has expressed her anger and frustration to Mrs Reed, and Bessie calls her "'a little roving, solitary thing'" (**p.71**) [**48**].

Her physical isolation is emphasised when she leaves Gateshead for Lowood: the porter's wife says to Bessie, "'What a long way! I wonder Mrs Reed is not afraid to trust her so far alone.'" (**p.74**) [**51**], and, on her arrival, Miss Temple comments, "'The child is very young to be sent alone'" (**p.75**) [**53**]. In the school garden Jane "... stood lonely enough: but to that feeling of isolation I was accustomed; it did not oppress me much" (**p.81**) [**59**] - a comment contradicted on page **101** [**81**], when she says to Helen Burns, "'I cannot bear to be solitary and hated'", though perhaps we are meant to understand by this that Jane can tolerate the physical isolation if it does not also involve emotional ostracization.

When Jane is travelling to Thornfield, we are told "It is a very strange sensation to inexperienced youth to feel itself quite alone in the world" (**p.125**) [**108**], and at Thornfield itself her isolation is emphasised when Rochester has guests and she, the governess, is either excluded from their gatherings or forced to sit in the room with them, but separate and apart. As a subordinate, but higher than a servant, she creeps into the drawing-room while the ladies and gentlemen are still at dinner to avoid drawing attention to herself (**p.199**) [**193**] or creeps down the back stairs, "issuing from my asylum with precaution" (**p.196**) [**190**] to seek food in the kitchen. Jane's arrival in Morton is marked by a number of references to her isolation: "... the white door closed, quite gently and civilly: but it shut me out" (**p.353**) [**367**] and, two paragraphs later, "I drew near houses; I left them and came back again, and again I wandered away: always repelled by the consciousness of having no claim to ask - no right to expect interest in my isolated lot." And, as she collapses on the steps of Moor House, "Alas, this isolation - this banishment from my kind!" (**p.361**) [**376**]. Jane has reached the depths of her loneliness and isolation.

It is interesting to explore the relationship betweeen Jane's isolation and her strong sense of independence. How responsible is she for her own isolation? How much is it the result of circumstances or other people?

Jane is not the only character in the novel to be isolated. Rochester is cut off from other people by his nature and circumstances, particularly his mad wife, a secret which he is at pains to keep from others. After the fire, he chooses to retire into even greater solitude, and his blindness further cuts him off from his fellow human-beings and the world about him. Both he and Jane are proud, and their pride fosters their desire for independence. Does it also isolate them?

St John Rivers is another isolated character. His desire for perfection and Christian martyrdom mark him out from his fellow men. Unable to tolerate weakness in himself, he is impatient of it in others, and his single-minded vocation allows for no relationships of any depth. Christ is his 'Master', as Rochester is Jane's. She escapes from her isolation in her love for Rochester. St John takes a more lonely road into the mission field.

Another character whom Charlotte Brontë presents to us as isolated is Helen Burns. Hers is the isolation of the saint. Modelled on Charlotte's oldest sister, Maria, who died at the age of eleven, she is marked out from her fellow pupils by her unworldly vision, her capacity for suffering, her love of learning and her pursuit of goodness. Hers is an isolation which appears to cause her no pain, because her sights are on heaven and the happiness of eternity. She is truly self-sufficient and holy in a way that St John is not. We sense, if we are not directly told by the author, that St John is spurred on in his search for holiness by a desire for martyrdom (In *Murder in the Cathedral* T.S. Eliot presents such a desire as a temptation for the Christian), and perhaps by an inadequacy in relating to his fellow human-beings. We warm to Helen, we don't to St John; but how much of our response to Helen is determined by her youth, the fact that she has consumption, and her early and poignant death?

Notes:

THE ROLE OF WOMEN (Q.6).

In *Jane Eyre* we see women in various categories (for want of a better word). There are those whose husbands and fathers are comfortably enough off to support them, like Mrs Reed and her daughters and like Rochester's visitors at Thornfield. In the case of the daughters of such households, they are usually busy looking for husbands, like Blanche Ingram, and much of the social activity they are involved in is with such an aim in mind. Their mothers' chief occupations are also to find husbands for their daughters.

At the other end of the social scale are the servants: the housekeeper, the cook, the maids. They are 'in service' because such work offered usually both a wage (minimal) and security (food and a roof over their heads) for women of the 'working classes'.

Between these two lies the group of women into which Jane herself fits and, indeed, into which the Brontë sisters fell. They are the women of what we might now call a 'middle-class' background, but whose fathers were not in a position to provide for them and had no prospect of doing so. They had enjoyed at least a limited education, which would have included probably some music and painting and drawing, perhaps a knowledge of a foreign language, together with sewing and embroidery. It was the education the Brontë sisters themselves had at the Parsonage and later at school in England and Brussels. It is the lot of women in this position that particularly interests Charlotte Brontë; they are the people whose role in life is most like her own.

Really the only career open to these women was as teachers, either in schools - like those at Lowood - or as governesses in big private houses, like Jane at Thornfield. Charlotte herself had been both. Neither position offered a woman any real independence; both were very badly paid. The role of the governess was an extremely lonely one: socially from a higher class than the servants, but inferior to her employers, she often found herself in a very isolated position. Jane's emotional isolatiom at Thornfield is alleviated, of course, by her intense love for Rochester, and also by the friendliness and kindness of Mrs Fairfax, who - like Nelly Dean in *Wuthering Heights* - to some extent bridges the wide gap between the other servants and the employer. It is clear, though, in the novel that young women like Jane had to learn to be very self-sufficient and to develop their own interests if they were to survive in such a situation. We see Jane finding her comfort and fulfilment in reading and in her drawing and painting, just as her cousins, Mary and Diana Rivers, do. They, we are told, are forced to go "as governesses in a large, fashionable, south-of-England city, where each held a situation in families by whose wealthy and haughty members they were regarded as humble dependants, and who neither knew nor sought one of their innate excellences, and appreciated only their acquired accomplishments as they appreciated the skill of their cook or the taste of their waiting-woman" (**p.379**) [**394**]. Jane's lot at Thornfield had been a great deal better than this; but it was not, of course, typical.

Given the lack of choice for women with no male relative to support them, it is not surprising that Jane greets the inheritance from her uncle with such delight - and relief - enabling her, as it does, to be financially independent. It was what the Brontë sisters themselves sought through their writing.

It is interesting to note that Mrs Gaskell, Charlotte Brontë's well-known friend and biographer, was preoccupied at the end of her life with providing a house for her unmarried daughters, so that they would not have to go away from home as governesses.

Notes:

PRINCIPLE AND NATURE (Q.7).

There is a sense in which we can see *Jane Eyre* as a novel about Jane's struggle to reconcile principle and nature. The first is variously called Reason, conscience, principle - that is, what she/one believes to be right; to obey Nature, on the other hand, is to do what one *feels* like doing. Jane has to fight against her natural instincts to obey her conscience, as we see throughout the novel.

At Gateshead, Jane, on the whole, obeys Nature, bursting out in rebellion against Mrs Reed and her injustice; but her very fight against injustice has its core in her sense of justice and her moral being, which belong to the realm of Principle.

At Lowood, Jane learns - through the examples of Helen Burns and Miss Temple and as she matures - to govern her natural temper and emotions, though her conversation with Helen on **page 101** [**81,82**] reveals her "impulsive", "vehement", "ardent" nature.

It is at Thornfield, however, that Jane faces the greatest conflict between Nature and Principle. Nature bids her sacrifice all her principles, her Christian conscience, and live with Rochester as his mistress. But Principle triumphs - at great cost to Jane. "In the midst of my pain of heart, and frantic effort of principle, I abhorred myself...As to my own will or conscience, impassioned grief had trampled one and stifled the other" (**p.348**) [**360**], she says after forcing herself to leave Thornfield and temptation behind her. By the time she is installed in her little cottage as schoolmistress at Morton, she has her emotions sufficiently under control to be able to say, "...I feel now that I was right when I adhered to principle and law, and scorned and crushed the insane promptings of a frenzied moment" (**p.386**) [**402**].

In St John Rivers, we see a man who has rejected Nature for Principle, just as Rochester had rejected Principle for Nature. St John says of himself, "'Reason, and not Feeling, is my guide'" (**p.401**) [**419**], and Jane fears if she marries him that she will be "...forced to keep the fire of my nature continually low, to compel it to burn inwardly and never utter a cry, though the imprisoned flame consumed vital after vital - *this* would be unendurable" (**p.433**) [**453**].

When Jane finds Rochester at Ferndean, she is able to reconcile Nature with Principle. Rochester is free to marry; indeed, he has behaved according to his conscience and Principle by risking his own life to save Bertha's. By learning to submit their passion, Nature, to Principle, they have earned the right to enjoy their love. (See Q.4).

Notes:

JANE EYRE, A 'MORAL' NOVEL (Q.8).

Much of the answer to the last question applies to this, also. Morality, of course, is concerned with distinguishing between right and wrong, with teaching what is right, according to conscience and Principle, and with seeing that right is rewarded and wrong punished.

Jane, throughout the novel, is concerned with doing right. As she matures at Lowood and at Thornfield, she becomes more conscious of what the right is, and it governs her behaviour both in relation to herself and to others.

Essentially, her sense of right is dictated by her Christian faith - her belief in God and in His judgement - though her relationship with Rochester clouds her own judgement, as she tells us in a warning passage on **page 302** [**307**]: "My future husband was becoming to me my whole world; and more than the world: almost my hope of heaven. He stood between me and every thought of religion, as an eclipse intervenes between man and the broad sun. I could not, in those days, see God for His creature: of whom I had made an idol." In the 'moral' novel, this tells us, she is not yet ready to enjoy Rochester's love. By the end of Chapter 26, however, when she is agonising over leaving Thornfield, she is aware again of God's presence: the 'eddying darkness' surrounds her, but "One idea only still throbbed life-like within me - a remembrance of God..." (**p.324**) [**331**]. She shares the basic moral code of her fellow 19th century Christians, but she is also very aware of her own human nature, including her need for emotional and sexual fulfilment, and knows it would be wrong to sacrifice these human needs to St John's fanatical vocation. The moral dilemma for Jane is how to marry Nature to Principle without sacrificing either. She finally resolves this at the end of the novel, as we have seen in the last question.

In her daily life, of course, the mature Jane leads what we would normally think of as a 'moral' life. She is honest, considerate of others, has a highly developed sense of duty towards those with whom she comes in contact, has learnt to forgive others as she hopes to be forgiven, even to the extent of visiting Mrs Reed on her deathbed and staying to comfort her daughters after her death.

In the novel, goodness and self-sacrifice are rewarded either in this world, as with Rochester and Jane and Diana and Mary Rivers, or in the next, as with Helen Burns and St John Rivers. Mrs Reed and her children are, by contrast, punished with unhappy and unfulfilled lives.

Notes:

JANE'S IMAGINATION (Q.9).

In the opening pages of the novel we are introduced to Jane as a highly sensitive, imaginative child. Reading Bewick's History of British Birds, she 'sees' the "bleak shores of Lapland, Siberia, Spitzbergen..." as Bewick describes them: "Of these death-white realms I formed an idea of my own; shadowy, like all the half-comprehended notions that float dim through children's brains, but strangely impressive. The words in these introductory pages connected themselves with the succeeding vignettes, and gave significance to the rock standing up alone in a sea of billow and spray; to the broken boat stranded on a desolate coast; to the cold and ghastly moon glancing through bars of cloud at a wreck just sinking" (**p.40**) [**14,15**].

This imaginative response to her reading prepares us for her challenge to John Reed, "'You are like a murderer - you are like a slave-driver - you are like the Roman Emperors!'" And she goes on to comment, "I had read Goldsmith's *History of Rome*, and had formed my opinion of Nero, Caligula, &c. Also, I had drawn parallels in silence, which I never thought thus to have declared aloud" (**p.43**) [**17**]. In the first few pages of the novel, then, we learn that Jane's imagination is fed by her reading. Through books she escapes from the cruel reality of life at Gateshead, and with their help she makes sense of what is happening to her: John Reed is a dictator, a Roman Emperor, a slave-driver.

By the time Jane is locked in the red-room, we are prepared for her imaginative response. When it grows dark and she sees a light gleaming on the wall, "...prepared as my mind was for horror, shaken as my nerves were by agitation, I thought the swift-darting beam was a herald of some coming vision from another world. My heart beat thick, my head grew hot; a sound filled my ears, which I deemed the rushing of wings: something seemed near me; I was oppressed, suffocated: endurance broke down - I uttered a wild, involuntary cry - I rushed to the door and shook the lock in desperate effort." And to Bessie she cries, "'Oh! I saw a light, and I thought a ghost would come'" (**p.49**) [**24, 25**]. To a child of her imaginative sensibility, in an over-wrought nervous state, surrounded by people who do not love her and whom she cannot trust, the experience of being locked in the red-room, where her uncle had died, marks a turning-point in Jane's life. The apothecary, called in to minister to Jane after the incident, intercedes on her behalf and she is sent away to school.

OTHER SUGGESTED REFERENCES

a)   At Lowood, when Jane's name has been cleared by Miss Temple in front of the whole school, she imagines herself becoming a competent painter and drawer and fluent in French - in short, developing the talents of a young lady: "I feasted…on the spectacle of ideal drawings, which I saw in the dark; all the work of my own hands: freely pencilled houses and trees, picturesque rocks and ruins, Cuyp-like groups of cattle, sweet paintings of butterflies hovering over unblown roses, of birds pecking at ripe cherries, of wrens' nests enclosing pearl-like eggs, wreathed about with young ivy sprays. I examined, too, in thought, the possibility of my ever being able to translate currently [fluently] a certain little French story-book which Madame Pierrot had that day shewn me" (**p.106**) [**87**]. What strikes us about this passage is the detail in which she imagines her aspirations being fulfilled.

b) On **page 143** [**128**], just before the first appearance of Rochester, Jane tells us, "In those days I was young, and all sorts of fancies bright and dark tenanted my mind: the memories of nursery stories were there amongst other rubbish; and when they recurred, maturing youth added to them a vigour and vividness beyond what childhood could give." She goes on to describe Pilot as "…one mask of Bessie's Gytrash", a North-of-England spirit, "…which, in the form of horse, mule, or large dog, haunted solitary ways, and sometimes came upon belated travellers…" It is worth noting here that Rochester shares Jane's vivid imagination. He later describes this first meeting with her, "'When you came on me in Hay lane last night, I thought unaccountably of fairy tales, and had half a mind to demand whether you had bewitched my horse'" (**p.153**) [**139**]. He repeatedly calls Jane 'elf', 'fairy' and sees her as appearing from another world.

c) On **page 190** [**182,183**] Jane tells us, "…I reviewed the information I had got; looked into my heart, examined its thoughts and feelings, and endeavoured to bring back with a strict hand such as had been straying through imagination's boundless and trackless waste, into the safe fold of common sense." Mrs Fairfax has told her about Blanche Ingram, and Jane, who is already falling in love with Rochester, is rebuking herself for dreaming of a possible future with him: "…a more fantastic idiot had never surfeited herself on sweet lies, and swallowed poison as if it were nectar." She has allowed her imagination to take control of 'Reason'.

d) When Rochester and Jane go shopping in Millcote for clothes for Jane in preparation for their marriage, Jane "…thought his smile was such as a sultan might, in a blissful and fond moment, bestow on a slave his gold and gems had enriched" (**p.297**) [**301**], and she tells him, "'I'll not stand you an inch in the stead of a seraglio…if you have a fancy for anything in that line, away with you, sir, to the bazaars of Stamboul without delay...'" (**p.297**) [**301,302**]. Again, her reading has fed her imagination, and it is interesting to note that, unconsciously, she realises that her relationship with Rochester is, at this stage, something like that of a slave to a master. She is right to be wary of Rochester's unlawful desire to own her, though she is unaware of the illegality at this stage. Later, of course, when they are free to marry, Jane sees their relationship as a liberating one, "To be together for us is to be at once as free as in solitude" (**p.476**) [**500**].

There are many other examples of Jane's imagination, of course, shown particularly in her paintings, in her dreams and, at the end, when she hears Rochester's voice calling her and responds by answering him and then seeking him out at Ferndean. Some of these we will look at when considering other questions.

Notes:

RESTRAINT AND SELF-DISCIPLINE (Q.10).

It is clear from the beginning of the novel that Jane values restraint and self-discipline, even when she feels unable to exercise it herself. After her outburst against Mrs Reed, she is "left there alone - winner of the field", but the sense of triumph does not last long, "A child cannot quarrel with its elders, as I had done; *cannot give its furious feelings uncontrolled play*, as I had given mine; without experiencing afterwards the pang of remorse and the chill of reaction" (**p.69**) [47].

At Lowood, under the influence particularly of Helen Burns and Miss Temple, she begins to learn the self-restraint which marks her as an adult. On **page 103** [**83**] we find her telling Miss Temple of Mrs Reed's injustice to her: "Exhausted by emotion, my language was more subdued than it generally was when it developed that sad theme; and mindful of Helen's warnings against the indulgence of resentment, I infused into the narrative far less of gall and wormwood than ordinary. *Thus restrained and simplified*, it sounded more credible: I felt as I went on that Miss Temple fully believed me." This is a very different Jane from the one we see at Gateshead: trusting and trusted, she is able to present what she feels passionately in a restrained and disciplined manner.

She practises the same restraint at Thornfield, when she forces herself to draw a portrait of Blanche Ingram and one of herself so that she can compare the two and see how unlikely it is that Rochester would choose her for a bride: "Ere long I had reason to congratulate myself on *the course of wholesome discipline* to which I had thus forced my feelings to submit: thanks to it, I was able to meet subsequent occurrences with a decent calm; which, had they found me unprepared, I should probably have been unequal to maintain even externally" (**p.191**) [**184**]. At the beginning of the following chapter she thinks about leaving Thornfield, "…involuntarily framing advertisements and pondering conjectures about new situations: these thoughts *I did not think it necessary to check*; they might germinate and bear fruit if they could" (**p.192**) [**185,186**]. It is clear from these two passages that Jane considers her feelings for Rochester in danger of getting out of control, whereas she can allow to go unchecked her practical thoughts about leaving Thornfield.

It is, of course, in her decision to leave Rochester that Jane shows the greatest restraint and self-discipline. In obeying Principle rather than Nature, she submits her natural passion to the restraint and discipline demanded by her Christian faith and its moral code.

Jane, of course, is not the only one to practise restraint. Helen Burns and Miss Temple both do so, Helen in pursuit of her Christian ideal and in the expectation of heaven, Miss Temple in the interests of her staff and pupils, implied rather than stated. St John Rivers, too, is a master of restraint and self-discipline, a point conveyed to us often through Charlotte Brontë's 'marble' images. Jane sees him as "'forging a fresh chain to fetter'" his heart (**p.399**) [**416**] and comments of him, "Reserved people often really need the frank discussion of their sentiments and griefs more than the expansive. The sternest-seeming stoic is human after all…" (**p.398**) [**416**].

The restraint of Helen Burns and St John Rivers she presents as belonging to another world than this. Helen tells Jane "'...God waits only the separation of spirit from flesh to crown us with a full reward. Why, then, should we ever sink overwhelmed with distress, when life is so soon over, and *death is so certain an entrance to happiness: to glory?'"* (**p.101**) [**82**]. And of St John Jane says at the end of the novel, "A more resolute, indefatigable pioneer never wrought amidst rocks and dangers... St. John is unmarried: he never will marry now. Himself has hitherto sufficed to the toil; and the toil draws near its close: his glorious sun hastens to its setting ... *he anticipated his sure reward, his incorruptible crown"* (**p.477**) [**501,2**].

As we look closely at the novel, we see the links between a number of the questions we have been discussing: the conflict between Nature and Principle is played out on a battlefield where passion and self-restraint are fighting. Charlotte Brontë never suggests that they are mutually exclusive; indeed, she suggests that a reconciliation of the two is essential for true happiness on this earth.

Notes:

EDUCATION (Q.11).

We can interpret the word 'education' in at least two ways when discussing *Jane Eyre*. In the usual, limited sense of the word, it refers to educational institutions or methods of learning: Lowood, the school at Morton of which Jane becomes schoolmistress, and her work as governess to Adèle all fit into this category. They provide an external structure to Jane's life; they also present us with considerable insight into the conditions of such institutions in nineteenth-century England. They tell us a great deal, for instance, about the harsh realities of the physical and emotional deprivation to be found in such charitable institutions as Lowood, of the loneliness and isolation of governesses, of the very limited educational opportunities available to girls in small rural communities such as Morton.

But *Jane Eyre* is also concerned with education in a wider sense, being "...what is sometimes called an education novel, showing the growth from childhood to maturity, tracing a development in moral insight and conduct", writes Barbara Hardy. It is about Jane's education in life, as well as her formal education in school and her role as an educator of others. She is, of course, in many ways self-educated, as the Brontë children themselves were. She has read widely, imaginatively (as we have seen), and intelligently before she goes to Lowood and receives formal teaching in such subjects as art and French.

But what attract Rochester to her are the qualities which she has developed in 'the school of life': her independence - in thought and action, her honesty, her refusal to flatter him. She has learnt to be her 'own person', as we might say now, because she has had to stand alone against injustice and isolation. She fascinates Rochester as something from another world, an elf, a fairy - as he tells Adèle on **page 296 [300]** - because he has inhabited a world where falseness and flattery are the norm. He has dissipated his naturally good qualities in a dissolute life ; he is living a lie at Thornfield and escapes from its confines as often as he can. He finds the reality of his situation unbearable. Jane, then, represents for him all that he is not (though they share a great deal, also, as we have seen): she accepts the reality of her situation with fortitude, she is honest, unflattering, reliable and independent. She has learnt to be these things, not simply through her formal education, though it has contributed, of course, but through her experiences in life, which she has turned to positive gain. Rochester, on the other hand, has allowed his experiences to embitter and corrupt him. He needs a good fairy to rescue him from himself!

Notes:

JANE EYRE, A RELIGIOUS NOVEL (Q.12)

Despite the criticisms of some of the early reviewers of *Jane Eyre*, particularly that in *Christian Remembrancer*, April 1848 (See Question 23), the novel can certainly be seen as 'religious', in at least two senses.

Most importantly, Jane herself is guided by Christian moral principles. She realises, as we have seen, that to allow Rochester to become more important to her than God is wrong. She leaves him because he already has a wife and for her to stay with him as his mistress would be in breach of Christian teaching. When she leaves Thornfield, she tells us "God must have led me on" and "May you never appeal to Heaven in prayers so hopeless and agonized as in that hour left my lips: for never may you, like me, dread to be the instrument of evil to what you wholly love" (**p.348**) [**361**]. She sees life in religious terms, in terms of good and evil, and it is her desire to follow the good that motivates her departure from Thornfield. There is no suggestion - stated or implied - that Charlotte Brontë does not approve her heroine's action.

In addition to Jane's own moral code, we are presented with two characters in the novel whose attitudes to life are those of committed, convinced Christians. They are, of course, Helen Burns and St John Rivers. Of Helen Burns there can be no doubt about her author's opinion. Modelled on Charlotte's eldest sister,

Maria, who died at the age of eleven, Helen is presented to us as an unselfish, idealistic, saintly child, whose true reward will be, as she expects, in heaven. Again, there is no suggestion that the author does not share her expectation of this reward. Quite the reverse.

St John Rivers is a more complicated character than Helen Burns, and Charlotte's attitude to him is obviously ambivalent. He is presented as a cold, restrained character, lacking human warmth and understanding, but in spite of the coldness they share (note the marble/pillar images), he has none of Mr Brocklehurst's sadism or hypocrisy. He dedicates his life to the mission field out of the highest ideals and, again, there is no suggestion that Charlotte Brontë does not think he deserves his reward in heaven.

While Jane's and Rochester's reward is here on earth, it is to be had only as a result of reconciling Nature with Principle, by following the Christian moral code of their time. Jane's resisting of temptation is a religious, as well as a moral, choice.

Notes:

THE GOTHIC (Q.13).

The term 'Gothic' in literature is often applied to works of poets and novelists writing in the Romantic period. Its characteristics are a sense of mystery, often relying on the past or things old for effect, a tendency to over-dramatization and melodrama, extravagance in description of place and feelings/emotions, particularly terror.

a) Jane's description of Thornfield Hall, as Mrs Fairfax first shows her to her room: "She took her candle, and I followed her from her room... The steps and bannisters were of oak; the staircase window was high and latticed: both it and the long gallery into which the bed-room doors opened, looked as if they belonged to a church rather than a house. A very chill and vault-like air pervaded the stairs and gallery, suggesting cheerless ideas of space and solitude..." (**p.129**) [**112,113**]. And she goes on to talk of "the eerie impression made by that wide hall, that dark and spacious staircase..."

The intention here is, of course, to make Thornfield seem mysterious and rather frightening to the new governess. The staircase window and the long gallery are even likened to a church, no doubt a Gothic church.

b) On **page 137** [**121**] Jane describes some of the third-story rooms: "...the imperfect light entering by their narrow casements showed bedsteads of a hundred years old; chests in oak or walnut, looking, with their strange carvings of palm branches and cherubs' heads, like types of the Hebrew ark...stools still more antiquated, on whose cushioned tops were yet apparent traces of half-effaced embroideries, wrought by fingers that for two generations had been coffin-dust. All these relics gave to the third story of Thornfield Hall the aspect of a home of the past: a shrine of memory."

Again, the mysterious, romantic sense of the past is tinged with mystery, "strange carvings", "Hebrew ark"; and the use of "coffin-dust" is very evocative, much more effective in immediacy than simply saying that the embroiderers had been dead for two generations.

c) The whole story of Bertha's imprisonment in the attic at Thornfield is Gothic in its intention and in its execution. The mystery which surrounds Grace Poole reaches its culmination, of course, in the scene where Bertha attacks her brother, and Jane has to watch over him until Rochester returns with the doctor (**pages 235ff.**) [**232ff.**]. We are told, "I must see the light of the unsnuffed candle wane on my employment; the shadows darken on the wrought, antique tapestry round me, and grow black under the hangings of the old bed, and quiver stangely over the the doors of a great cabinet opposite..." (**p.239**) [**237**].

The whole atmosphere, conveyed in such descriptions, together with the use of such words as "wild beast", "fiend", "snarling, canine noise" to describe the mad woman, contribute to creating a Gothic scene of melodrama, suspense and terror.

d) Jane's approach to Ferndean at the end of the novel offers another opportunity for Gothic description. The house is "deep buried in a wood"; iron gates, granite pillars and branched arches, together with the darkness, (**p.455**) [**478**] all suggest mystery and foreboding.

It is worth noting that Robert Heilman, in his essay *Charlotte Brontë's 'New' Gothic in* **Jane Eyre** *and* **Villette** (Casebook Series), sees Charlotte Brontë's use of the Gothic as much more complex and less conventional than it has usually been considered. We have not dealt with his views here.

Notes:

THE SUPERNATURAL (Q.14).

The supernatural is often linked to the Gothic, since it is a favourite device for creating a sense of mystery as well as introducing fear/terror. It often depends, also, of course, on the past - ghosts and haunted houses are obvious examples of this.

There are many examples of the use of the supernatural in *Jane Eyre*. These are just a few of them:

a)   In the red-room Jane thinks the light on the wall is "a herald of some coming vision from another world" (**p.49**) [**24**]. It is her fear of her uncle's ghost - he had died and been laid out in the room - that causes her terror.

b)   Rochester constantly talks of Jane as a being from another world. In this case, the references to the supernatural are not frightening, but pleasing, exciting, surprising. She is his "fairy" (**pp.273,296,461,463**) [**276,300,485,487**]; she is an "elf" or comes from "Elf-land" (**pp.272,287,296,302**) [**275,290,300,307**]; she is his "good genii" (**p.182**) [**171**], his "sprite" (**p.302**) [**307**], his "changeling" (**pp.302,463**) [**307,487**]. On **page 306** [**311**] he tells her, "…you are dripping like a mermaid…"

c)   In addition to the fairy/elf images, Jane is a "witch, sorceress" (**pp.180,299,309**) [**169,303,314**], and Rochester is "bewitched" by her (**p.452**) [**474**].

d)   Bertha is variously described as a "goblin" (**p.336**) [**348**] and "cunning as a witch" (**p.452**) [**475**]. Note the difference in tone and effect between this critical reference to Bertha as a witch and Rochester's teasing, loving challenge when he calls Jane by that name.

e)   When Jane looks at the clothes Rochester has bought her for her wedding, she cannot believe they are real, as she cannot believe she will be Mrs Rochester. She refers to the "wraith-like apparel" and the "ghostly shimmer" of the clothes (**p.303**) [**308**]. These references to the supernatural are ominous, of course: they suggest the unreality of her situation and reflect her unconscious fears.

f)   On **page 444** [**467**] Jane hears Rochester calling her and responds by telling him, "'I am coming! …Wait for me!'" and then "'Where are you?'" We could read this as simply Jane's imagination and her response to it; but on **page 471** [**496, 497**] we learn that the words Jane hears are the ones spoken by Rochester, and he, in return, hears exactly what she says. Jane decides not to tell Rochester of these details at the time as "that mind, yet from its sufferings too prone to gloom, needed not the deeper shade of the supernatural." This incident is an experience of the supernatural which is in another category, of course, from the references we have listed above.

g) Jane's dream of the ruin of Thornfield Hall (**p.310**) [**316**] could also be seen as a supernatural premonition. It precedes the Gothic description of Bertha's appearance in Jane's room and her attack on her wedding veil, like "the Vampyre" (**p.311**) [**317**]. The dream suggests Jane's unconscious fears that she will lose Rochester and the security and hope which his love represents to her.

Notes:

DREAMS (Q.15).

At the beginning of Chapter 21 Jane comments specifically on dreaming of children. She cites her old nurse Bessie claiming that to dream of children was "a sure sign of trouble, either to one's self or one's kin". And Jane goes on to talk of her own dreams - of their frequency and their alarming nature.

a) The dreams referred to on **page 249** [**248**] are all of "...an infant: which I sometimes hushed in my arms, sometimes dandled on my knee, sometimes watched playing with daisies on a lawn...whatever aspect it wore, it failed not for seven successive nights to meet me the moment I entered the land of slumber." Jane goes on to say that one of these dreams preceded the incident in which Bertha attacks Mason, and Jane is called upon to help and stay with Mason on 'the fateful third story' (**p.237**) [**234,235**]. It is on the day following this that she is brought news of John Reed's death and Mrs Reed's illness (**pp.249,250**) [**248,249**].

b) On **page 309** [**315**] Jane tells Rochester of a dream she has had in his absence: "'...I continued in dreams the idea of a dark and gusty night. I continued also the wish to be with you, and experienced a strange, regretful consciousness of some barrier dividing us. During all my first sleep, I was following the windings of an unknown road; total obscurity environed me; rain pelted me; I was burdened with the charge of a litttle child: a very small creature, too young and feeble to walk, and which shivered in my cold arms, and wailed piteously in my ear. I thought, sir, that you were on the road a long way before me; and I strained every nerve to overtake you and made effort on effort to utter your name and entreat you to stop - but my movements were fettered; and my voice still died away inarticulate; while you, I felt, withdrew farther and farther every moment.'"

It is not difficult to see, in this dream, how Jane's unconscious fears are working. She has heard Bessie's account of how dreams of children augur ill, so the child here suggests misfortune. Rochester's temporary absence triggers off fears of a more permanent one. Jane's experience of the loss of everything dear to her in life - her parents, Helen Burns, even Miss Temple in marriage - has conditioned her to *expect* the loss of what she loves. Notice phrases like "strained every nerve" and "made effort on effort" and "my movements were fettered" as she attempts to reach Rochester: it is what she wants most of all, yet he "withdrew farther and farther every moment".

c) Jane goes on to tell Rochester of another dream, the one we have looked at briefly at the end of the last question (14g).

In it, "'Thornfield Hall was a dreary ruin, the retreat of bats and owls. I thought that of all the stately front nothing remained but a shell-like wall, very high and very fragile-looking...Wrapped up in a shawl I still carried the unknown little child. I might not lay it down anywhere, however tired were my arms - however much its weight impeded my progress, I must retain it. I heard the gallop of a horse at a distance on the road: I was sure it was you; and you were departing for many years, and for a distant country...'" (**p.310**) [**316**]. The account continues with a description of Jane's "frantic perilous haste" to catch "one glimpse of you"; the child "almost strangled me" and Rochester is "like a speck on a white track, lessening every moment".

Again, we see the great fear of loss, the burden of the child (her fear perhaps?), the lost Rochester, the frantic effort to reach him. The ruined Thornfield can be seen as the loss of Rochester and of her home (See Question 1 - arguably as important as love to Jane), but also as a premonition of what is to happen in reality, when the Hall is destroyed by fire. Ironically, of course, the destruction of Thornfield brings the death of Bertha and leaves Rochester and Jane free to marry.

Notes:

CLOTHES AND PHYSICAL APPEARANCE (Q.16).

The novel is full of references to clothes and characters' appearances. They are there, of course, to enable the reader to visualize the people Charlotte Brontë creates, but they have a more symbolic role to play. They are instrumental in suggesting the kind of character she is presenting to us. After all, when we have a choice, we choose the clothes we wear according to our own image of ourselves, even if that is partly dictated by current fashion.

a)   On **page 76** [**53**] the girls at Lowood are described as "uniformly dressed in brown stuff frocks of quaint fashion, and long holland pinafores". What this description tells us is that the pupils have no say about what they wear, and they are dressed in plain, unattractive, rather old-fashioned (quaint) clothing to emphasise the fact that they are in a charitable institution and must not have ideas above their station in life. On **page 79** [**57**] Jane adds to this description, concluding "Above twenty of those clad in this costume were full-grown girls; or rather young women: it suited them ill, and gave an air of oddity even to the prettiest."

b)   In ironical contrast to the girls, the Misses Brocklehurst arrive at the school with "gray beaver hats, then in fashion, shaded with ostrich plumes, and from under the brim of this graceful headdress fell a profusion of light tresses, elaborately curled...", and their mother is "enveloped in a costly velvet shawl, trimmed with ermine", and is wearing "a false front of French curls" (**p.97**) [**76**]. Just before this description Mr Brocklehurst has ordered the natural curls of one of the Lowood girls to be 'cut off entirely' (**p.96**) [**75,6**]. Note the contrast between the 'natural' curls and 'the false front of French curls'. Mr Brocklehurst's wife and daughters dress with the ostentation and insensitivity to the situation that we would expect of his family. Charlotte Brontë comments, "They ought to have come a little sooner to have heard his lecture on dress, for they were splendidly attired in velvet, silk, and furs" (**p.97**) [**76**].

c)   On Jane's first morning at Thornfield, we are told, "...I dressed myself with care: obliged to be plain - for I had no article of attire that was not made with extreme simplicity - I was still by nature solicitous to be neat. It was not my habit to be disregardful of appearance, or careless of the impression I made: on the contrary, I ever wished to look as well as I could, and to please as much as my want of beauty would permit" (**p.130**) [**113**]. She goes on to say how often she wishes she were 'handsomer' but concludes, "However, when I had brushed my hair very smooth, and put on my black frock - which, Quaker-like as it was, at least had the merit of fitting to a nicety - and adjusted my clean white tucker, I thought I should do respectably enough to appear before Mrs Fairfax..."

This description of Jane reinforces the impression we have already formed of her: she is never ostentatious in her dress, just as she prefers to remain inconspicuous in a crowd. She is reserved, but stong-minded and independent, and her neat, matter-of-fact and business-like dress suggests these elements in her character. We learn elsewhere of her "black merino cloak, a black beaver bonnet" (**p.146**), [131] and, asked to take tea with Rochester, "...I repaired to my room, and, with Mrs Fairfax's aid, replaced my black stuff dress by one of black silk; the best and the only additional one I had, except one of light grey, which, in my Lowood notions of the toilette, I thought too fine to be worn, except on first-rate occasions" (**p.151**) [136].

d) In contrast with Jane, Rochester's visitors appear flamboyantly dressed in blue and azure, crimson and gold, and 'spotless white' (**pp.200-202**) [**194-196**]. Fashionable and 'showy', they dress to make an impression and to draw attention to themselves.

e) Adèle, by nature, wants to belong to this fashionable world, and we see this desire reflected in her interest in the visitors, her anxiety to be part of their social evenings, and in her interest in her own appearance. On **page 170**, [**158**] her "little foot was heard tripping across the hall. She entered, transformed, as her guardian had predicted. A dress of rose-coloured satin, very short, and as full in the skirt as it could be gathered, replaced the brown frock she had previously worn; a wreath of rosebuds circled her forehead; her feet were dressed in silk stockings and small white satin sandals.

'Est-ce que ma robe va bien?' cried she, bounding forwards; 'et mes souliers? et mes bas?...'" And on another occasion, Jane tells her, "'You think too much of your 'toilette', Adèle'", and turns her face away to "conceal a smile I could not suppress: there was something ludicrous as well as painful in the little Parisienne's earnest and innate devotion to matters of dress" (**p.200**) [**194**]. The word "innate" reminds us, of course, of Adèle's parentage, of her unfaithful (to Rochester) French mother.

Notes:

PICTURES AND PAINTINGS (Q.17).

The references to and descriptions of pictures, paintings and of painting and drawing in *Jane Eyre* have several different functions in the novel. Let's look at some of these in the following examples:

a) In Chapter 1, as we have already seen, Jane is reading and looking at the illustrations in Bewick's *History of British Birds*. She says quite frankly that she was not very interested in the text, except for "certain introductory pages" - what interests her in them, she goes on to tell us, are the 'romantic', Gothic descriptions of "the haunts of sea-fowl" and "the bleak shores" of Lapland, etc. "The words in these introductory pages connected themselves with the succeeding vignettes", she continues, and tells us what some of these pictures contain: a "rock standing up alone in a sea of billow and spray", a "broken boat stranded on a desolate coast", a "cold and ghastly moon glancing through the bars of cloud at a wreck just sinking" (**p.40**) [**14,15**]. She goes on with further descriptions, all of which testify to her vivid and romantic imagination - romantic in the sense of idealised, scenes chosen for their imaginative, rather than realistic appeal.

What this whole passage conveys to us, then, is Jane's imaginative nature. She likes pictures which suggest to her a story, "Each picture told a story; mysterious often to my undeveloped understanding and imperfect feelings, yet ever profoundly interesting..." (**pp.40,41**) [**15**]. Through these stories, she escapes, then, from the reality of life with the Reeds at Gateshead into an imaginative world of her own.

b) On **page 157** [**142,143**] Jane describes in detail watercolours she has painted and is showing Rochester, at his request. Like Bewick's engravings, they are highly imaginative, Gothic, mysterious, with their rendering of stormy seas, lurid lights, strange isolated figures. Rochester says of them, "As to the thoughts, they are elfish" (**p.158**) [**144**]. (Margaret Smith in her note on this passage in the Oxford University Press World's Classics edition of *Jane Eyre* refers us to an article by Jane Stedman in Brontë Society *Transactions*, 1966, in which the writer explores "the likeness between these paintings and the engravings in Bewick's *British Birds*"; and Margaret Smith herself reminds us that "'Livid' or storm-torn clouds and swollen seas were also characteristic of the painter John Martin, whose work much impressed Charlotte Brontë"). These paintings, then, further testify to Jane's vivid imagination and also to her need to express that imaginative world in the midst of her drab and monotonous 'real' one. We are making no attempt here to interpret any of these paintings, though that is an interesting exercise.

c) When Jane is recalled to Gateshead after the death of John Reed, she spends much of her time drawing. The pictures she at first describes (**p.261**) [**262**] are very like the ones previously mentioned and serve clearly as a means of escape from a place and people uncongenial to her. Her preoccupation with and love for Rochester are, of course, reflected in her portrait of him, which she goes on to draw, almost unconsciously, "One morning I fell to sketching a face: what sort of a face it was to be I did not care or know" (**p.261**) [**262**].

d) At Moor House Diana and Mary Rivers are impressed by Jane's drawing and painting; she gives them lessons in art, and they teach her German. Clearly, here, her artistic skills and education are a means of showing her equality with the Rivers family: they share the same interests, and she is worthy of being their friend and cousin. Similarly, her sketch of Rosamond Oliver, as well as providing insight into St John, serves as an entrée to Vale-Hall (**p.395**) [**412,413**].

It is interesting to note that all the drawings and paintings we have looked at are executed when Jane is unhappy or unfulfilled, either before she meets Rochester or when she thinks she has lost him. And at Thornfield, where she is generally happy, the only detailed descriptions of her art are inspired by her jealousy of Blanche Ingram and her need to face what she sees as the reality of losing Rochester to Blanche (**pp.190,191**) [**183,184**]. In her essay, *Art and the Artist as Heroine in the Novels of Charlotte, Emily and Anne Brontë,* Jane Sellars has some very interesting things to say about the importance of art and the significance of the artist in *Jane Eyre.*

Notes:

NATURE (Q.18).

Charlotte Brontë uses Nature, the natural world, in several different ways in *Jane Eyre*. Sometimes it is there for a) straight literal description of background or foreground, but often it is used symbolically: b) to suggest the mood or character of a person, or c) as a contrast with the feelings of one of the characters; sometimes it is used d) to reinforce the metaphorical significance of place. It is not always easy to distinguish between these different functions; indeed, they often seem to overlap.

When Jane meets Rochester for the first time, she has been walking along a lane "...noted for wild roses in summer, for nuts and blackberries in autumn, and even now possessing a few coral treasures in hips and haws; but whose best winter delight lay in its utter solitude and leafless repose" (**p.142**) [**127**]. This, it seems, is a literal description of the place where Jane and Rochester meet - an important moment which needs to be firmly rooted in place. One could, of course, also see a symbolic intention: it is, though not at the moment, a fruitful, fertile place, as Jane's and Rochester's relationship is going to be fruitful when they have survived the 'winter' of their suffering and separation.

In the same way, when Jane is wandering at Whitcross, we are given a detailed description of the countryside in which she finds herself, so that we can visualize her there. In addition to this important function, however, we are aware that the natural world reflects her sense of loneliness and anxiety. The moors surround her on all sides, the roads stretch 'white, broad, and lonely'. "If a gust of wind swept the waste, I looked up, fearing it was the rush of a bull; if a plover whistled, I imagined it a man" (**p.349**) [**363**]. Her fears, then, are seen in natural terms, and so are her feelings of confidence as night falls. "Nature seemed to me benign and good: I thought she loved me, outcast as I was", she says on **page 350 [363]**. In this passage, then, it seems that Charlotte Brontë is using nature literally, but also symbolically to reflect Jane's feelings and to emphasise her loneliness through the isolation of the place.

The descriptions of Gateshead at the beginning of the novel fulfil the same function: they establish the place literally, but, dominated by images of bitter cold and rain - the frosty windows, the hungry robin on the leafless cherry-tree - they also reinforce for us the metaphorical coldness and hunger of Jane's own loveless life with the Reed family.

By contrast, at the beginning of Chapter 9, Jane describes the coming of spring to Lowood: "...the privations, or rather the hardships of Lowood lessened. Spring drew on...the frosts of winter had ceased; its snows were melted; its cutting winds ameliorated...we could now endure the play-hour passed in the garden: sometimes on a sunny day it began even to be pleasant and genial, and a greenness grew over those brown beds which, freshening daily, suggested the thought that Hope traversed them at night, and left each morning brighter traces of her steps..." (**p.**107) [**88**]. And she continues, "...Lowood shook loose its tresses; it became all green, all flowery; its great elm, ash, and oak skeletons were restored to magic life; woodland plants sprang up profusely in its recesses..." The coming of spring reflects Jane's own hopes and delight in her new-found freedom. There is irony here, too, of course, because the liberty she is enjoying is because there is an outbreak of typhus in the school and rules have been relaxed. The images of new life in the natural world - the 'skeletons' of the trees coming alive - are in bitter contrast to the images of death, a fact which Jane is to be brought face-to-face with at the death of Helen Burns, though she dies of consumption, not of the typhus epidemic sweeping the school.

As in the novels of Thomas Hardy, Charlotte Brontë sometimes implies the indifference which Nature shows towards the affairs of men. On **page 248 [246]**, Jane tells us, "He paused: the birds went on carolling, the leaves lightly rustling. I almost wondered they did not check their songs and whispers to catch the suspended revelation..." In Hardy's novels, the indifference of Nature is usually to more dramatic, tragic circumstances in the characters' lives than we see here.

Perhaps the most memorable use of Nature as symbol is found at the end of Chapter 26, when Jane has learnt of Rochester's marriage. The passage beginning, "Jane Eyre, who had been an ardent, expectant woman..." (**pp.**323,324) [**330,331**] is an extended natural metaphor, in which she sees what has happened as the coming of a bitter cold December to the June of her happiness. It is followed by the equally memorable description of the great torrents of water - symbolising her sense of 'love lost...hope quenched' - descending on her in a mighty rush.

Both St John and Rochester are described in natural metaphors: St John is "fixed as a rock, firm set in the depths of a restless sea" (**p.**400) [**418**] and Rochester in his dependence on Jane is likened to "...a royal eagle, chained to a perch...forced to entreat a sparrow to become its purveyor" (**p.**464) [**488**]. Jane, by contrast, is his 'sky-lark' (**p.**464) [**488**], as she has been his 'dove' (**p.**337) [**348**] and his 'linnet' (**p.**339) [**351**].

There are many other natural references, images and metaphors in the novel, notably the chestnut-tree, and some of these will be looked at under their own headings in the next question.

Notes:

IMAGERY (Q.19).

a)   *Fire/Heat.*

There are many references to fire or heat in the novel. Sometimes, of course, it is used literally, as part of a description of a room, where it is a focal point; but it is very often used metaphorically, even in this connection, to suggest comfort, safety, home. We see this when Jane first arrives at Thornfield, "...she ushered me into a room, whose double illumination of fire and candle at first dazzled me, contrasting as it did with the darkness to which my eyes had been for two hours inured; when I could see, however, a cozy and agreeable picture presented itself to my view. A snug, small room; a round table by a cheerful fire." (**p.127**) [**110**] And Mrs Fairfax greets her with, "'...you must be cold, come to the fire'" and, a little later on **page 127** [**111**], "'Now, then, draw nearer to the fire'".

Of this introduction to Thornfield, Jane thinks, "'I little expected such a reception; I anticipated only coldness and stiffness...'" (**p.128**) [**111**]. Clearly, she is talking here not of the literal fire which warms her physically and dispels the literal cold, but of what it stands for: the warmth and comfort of home and security. The 'genial fire' that heralds Rochester's arrival home (**p.148**) [**133**] serves the same purpose. He is going to find Thornfield a much more 'congenial' place/home now that Jane is there.

Fire is also used in the novel as a metaphor for passion. On **page 226** [**222**], when Rochester is disguised as an old gipsy woman, he tells Jane, "'...You are cold; because you are alone: no contact strikes the fire from you that is in you...'" He is trying to make her aware, of course, of his own passion for her - "'...nor will you stir one step to meet it where it waits you...'" - and also to persuade her to ackowledge her passion for him.

On **page 267** [**269**], Mrs Reed rebukes Jane, "'...how for nine years you could be patient and quiescent under any treatment, and in the tenth break out all fire and violence, I can never comprehend'", she says of Jane's passionate outbursts against her and her son.

When Helen Burns is punished by having to wear a piece of pasteboard, Jane "...ran to Helen, tore it off, and thrust it into the fire: the fury of which she was incapable had been *burning* in my soul all day, and tears, hot and large, had continually been *scalding* my cheek..." (**pp.105, 106**) [**86**]. The literal fire burns the pasteboard, but the metaphorical fire of righteous anger burns Jane.

These are just a few of the fire images to be found in *Jane Eyre*. Some other examples - by no means all - are: "'...a solemn passion... *kindling in pure, powerful flame*, fuses you and me in one...'" (**p.342**) [**354**]; "He seemed to devour me with his *flaming* glance: physically, I felt, at the moment, powerless as stubble exposed to the draught and glow of a *furnace*" (**p.344**) [**356**]; "forth *flashed the fire* from his eyes" (**p. 345**) [**358**]; "the redness and radiance of a *glowing peat-fire*" at Moor House (**p.358**) [**372**]; "I saw his solemn eye melt with sudden *fire*, and *flicker* with resistless emotion. Flushed and *kindled* thus, he looked nearly as beautiful for a man as she for a woman" (**p.390**) [**407**]; " . . . the hope of passing a lifetime at his side, would be renewed, with all its first force and *fire* (**p.393**) [**410**]; " . . . forced to keep the fire of my nature continually low, to compel it to *burn* inwardly and never utter a cry, though the imprisoned *flame* consumed vital after vital..." (**p.433**) [**453**].

b) Cold.

As with the images of fire and heat, those of cold can be both literal and metaphorical in *Jane Eyre*. Indeed, images of heat and cold are often juxtaposed, as we have already seen.

The cold of a Lowood winter, described at the beginning of Chapter 6, accentuates, of course, not only the physical cold, but also the lack of human warmth and comfort that the girls experience. We have already commented on the symbolic use of "all was still and petrified under the influence of a hard frost" at Gateshead (**p.62**) [**39**]. Contrast both of these descriptions, for instance, with the welcome which Jane receives at Thornfield, with its emphasis on the 'cheerful' fire (**p.127**) [**110**].

We have also seen how, when Jane's name is cleared by Miss Temple, and she has begun to be accepted at Lowood, "...the frosts of winter had ceased; its snows were melted..." (**p.107**) [**88**]. She is describing the coming of spring, but she is also referring to a change in her feelings about the place.

When Rochester is trying to persuade Jane not to leave him, after the revelation of his marriage, he anticipates how she will blame and reject him, "'...you will say, - 'That man had nearly made me his mistress: I must be ice and rock to him'; and ice and rock you will accordingly become'" (**p.327**) [**338**]. The coldness of manner and emotion which Rochester fears here is like the iciness of St John, depicted on **pages** 437 and 438 [**459**], when he anticipates Jane's refusal to marry him, "Reader, do you know, as I do, what terror those cold people can put into the ice of their questions? How much of the fall of the avalanche is in their anger? of the breaking up of the frozen sea in their displeasure?".

As with the images of fire, there are many of cold in the novel. Some others are: On St John's arrival in the snow at Jane's small cottage at Morton, his tall figure is 'all white as a *glacier*' (**p.403**) [**421**]; "I began to feel he had spoken truth of himself, when he said he was hard and *cold*" (**p.418**) [**438**]; "...his reserve was again *frozen* over" (**p.421**) [**441**]; "...I fell under a *freezing* spell (**p.423**) [**443**]; "There are no such things as marble kisses, or *ice* kisses, or I should say, my ecclesiastical cousin's salute belonged to one of these classes" (**p.424**) [**444**]. Note how many of these cold images refer to St John. With the stone and marble images, which he shares with Mr

Brocklehurst, they combine to portray him as a man lacking warmth and passion.

c) Books.

The first sight we have of Jane is of her with a book. Throughout the novel books represent a means of escape and food for her imagination. The escape is not only a momentary one, as at the beginning of *Jane Eyre*; it is through reading and education that she will escape the servitude and dependence which she dreads. Books and learning in general will form a bond, also, with Helen Burns, Rochester and her Rivers cousins.

We have already seen how books feed Jane's imagination. It is interesting to note that the first time we meet Helen Burns, she, too, is reading; but her interest is very different from Jane's, being more intellectual than imaginative. Jane rejects *Rasselas* because "I saw nothing about fairies, nothing about genii..." (**p.82**) [**60**]. Nevertheless, they share a common interest in reading, and it forms a bond between them.

On **pages 376** and 377 [**392**], Jane says of the Rivers sisters, "They were both more accomplished and better read than I was: but with eagerness I followed in the path of knowledge they had trodden before me. I devoured the books they lent me: then it was full satisfaction to discuss with them in the evening what I had perused during the day. Thought fitted thought; opinion met opinion: we coincided, in short, perfectly".

Compare this passage with, "St John had a book in his hand - it was his unsocial custom to read at meals..." (**p.421**) [**440**] and the description of how, when he is teaching Jane Hindustanee, he "took away my liberty of mind" (**p.423**) [**443**] and "held me in thrall" (**p.424**) [**444**]. Books and learning are not shared with St John as they are with his sisters.

And at the end of the novel Jane says of Rochester, "He saw nature - he saw books through me" and "Never did I weary of reading to him" (**p.476**) [**500**].

With all the people to whom Jane is attracted, she shares a common interest in reading and books. They are her passport into a country which would otherwise be denied her, both imaginatively and literally.

d)   Stone.

The images of stone in the novel are most frequently used to suggest the coldness and inflexibility of Mr Brocklehurst and, particularly, St John Rivers; but occasionally they are used in connection with Rochester and even Jane, as we shall see in the following examples:

Most obviously, Mr Brocklehurst is "a black pillar" and his "grim face at the top was like a carved mask" (**p.63**) [**40**]. The "black column" image is reiterated on **page 94** [**73**], when he comes to Lowood, and on **page 98** [**78**] he is referred to as "the black marble clergyman". He has the stiffness, the coldness of a stone pillar, and the black suggests perhaps the fear he engenders in Jane and the evil of his sadistic nature.

St John shares the 'marble' image with Mr Brocklehurst. There are numerous examples of this in the last part of the novel. He is shown "maintaining a marble immobility of feature" on **page 383** [**399**], "his marble-seeming features" are referred to on **page 393** [**411**], and "that marble breast" on **page 397** [**415**]. His kiss is like marble (**p.424**) [**444**] and his heart like 'stone' (**p.436**) [**458**]. His nature is cold, lacking in warmth and flexibility; but he is not an evil man, so the marble is never black when the image is used of St John.

When Rochester's marriage to Bertha is revealed, "...how like quarried marble was his pale, firm massive front..." and "His whole face was colourless rock: his eye was both spark and flint" (**p.318**) [**324**]. The suggestion here, surely, is that, Rochester, faced with the loss of Jane, is filled with a rock-like determination to hold on to her. The image also suggests, of course, the rock-like strength of Rochester's character, which represents such security to Jane. In the light of the image used when Jane is looking at the ruin of Thornfield and wondering whether Rochester is dead - "'Is he with Damer de Rochester, sharing the shelter of his narrow marble house?'" (**p.450**) [**473**] - we might ask whether the earlier use of the marble image does not suggest the death to all his hopes and desires which Rochester fears if he loses Jane, just as the image of Jane lying "motionless as a stone" (**p.365**) [**379**] on her bed at Moor House suggests the death-like loss of *her* hopes.

e) Moon.

The moon or moon-light is used frequently in the novel to indicate the literal light which brightens up the darkness, as when Jane is looking for Helen Burns in Miss Temple's room, "...the light of the unclouded summer moon...enabled me to find it without difficulty" (**p.111**) [**93**]. Even here, though, there may be irony: the 'unclouded' moon is leading her to the death of Helen.

The moon is also used symbolically in *Jane Eyre* to suggest mystery and romance: "...the moon was waxing bright' (**p.145**) [**129**] when Jane met Rochester in Hay lane, and she tells him "'I am not at all afraid of being out late when it is moonlight'" (**p.145**) [**130**]. On her way back to Thornfield, "I saw only the hedge and a pollard willow before me, rising up to meet the moonbeams" (**p.147**) [**132**], and she goes on to say, "I did not like re-entering Thornfield. To pass its threshold was to return to stagnation" (**p.147**) [**132**]. To the moon belongs the magical, fanciful, romantic world of her meeting with Rochester, which she is reluctant to leave. Ironically, of course, her re-entry to Thornfield is not "to return to stagnation", but she does not know yet that Rochester is master of the Hall.

At the end of the novel, Rochester reinforces this use of the moon image by saying to Jane, "'...our honey-moon will shine our life-long: its beams will only fade over your grave or mine'" (**p.475**) [**499**].

f) Storm.

The images of storm, which include those of wind and rain and snow, are to be found throughout the novel. They fulfil various functions: they are a metaphor for passion, they echo the upheaval going on in the characters' lives; sometimes they forecast that upheaval, are an omen that all will not be well.

On **page 173** [**161**] Rochester tells Jane that one day she will know what passion is. In the passage beginning, "Floating on with closed eyes" he tells her "'...you will come some day to a craggy pass of the channel, where the whole of life's stream will be broken up into whirl and tumult, foam and noise: either you will be dashed to atoms on crag-points, or lifted up and borne on by some master wave into a calmer current...'" He forecasts the emotional storm which awaits her, of course, when she learns he is already married.

After his proposal to her (**p.284**) [**287**], Jane comments, "And what ailed the chestnut-tree? it writhed and groaned; while wind roared in the laurel walk, and came sweeping over us." A violent thunder-storm follows, in which the tree is struck by lightning. The whole scene augurs that all will not be well with the engaged couple. So does the 'blast' in her dream of the ruin of Thornfield Hall (**p.310**) [**316**].

Both when she arrives at Lowood - "I heard a wild wind rushing amongst trees" (**p.74**) [**52**] - and when she approaches Moor House - "...the night wind swept over the hill...the rain fell fast" (**p.357**) [**371**] - Jane is exposed to the elements, reflecting the upheaval in her life and in her emotions.

Again, when St John comes to tell Jane he has discovered her true identity, he arrives in a 'whirling storm' (**p.403**) [**421**]. The 'keen wind' brings 'fresh and blinding falls' of snow, and St John appears out of 'the howling darkness'. The news he brings (that she is their cousin and their uncle's heir) is, of course, of enormous emotional - as well as financial - importance to Jane (and St John), and the storm reflects this.

The storm images, while fulfilling a metaphorical function, also contribute in a literal way to establishing setting and atmosphere: they create tension, dramatic intensity and a sense of mystery and expectation.

g) *Water.*

Water, without which there can be no life, is a traditional symbol of life itself, of hope. The water images in *Jane Eyre* are mostly traditional ones of this sort, though there are occasional exceptions.

When spring comes to Lowood, Jane discovers outside the "high and spike-guarded walls" of the garden "...a bright beck, full of dark stones and sparkling eddies" (**p.107**) [**88**]. It suggests, of course, her new-found freedom and hope (she has just personified Hope to emphasise its importance for her).

Likewise, when she is about to meet Rochester in Hay lane, she becomes aware of the noise of the "many becks" (**p.143**) [**128**]; and the bustle of life at Thornfield once he has arrived is described in metaphorical terms: "...a rill from the outer world was flowing through it; it had a master: for my part, I liked it better" (**p.150**) [**135**] . Both these suggest the new life and hope which Rochester's arrival bring to Jane's existence.

In the last paragraph of Chapter 15 (**p.182**) [**172**] we find a more complex use of the image: "I was tossed on a buoyant but unquiet sea, where billows of trouble rolled under surges of joy..." Here the sea can be both buoyant and joyous, bringing life and hope; but it can also be "wild" and unquiet in danger of drowning her.

The most forceful image in this category comes, of course, at the end of Chapter 26, after the revelation of Rochester's marriage. Here "...I seemed to have laid me down in the dried-up bed of a great river; I heard a flood loosened in remote mountains, and felt the torrent come", and she concludes with an adaptation of the beginning of Psalm 69: "'the waters came into my soul; I sank in deep mire: I felt no standing; I came into deep waters; the floods overflowed me'" (**p.324**) [**331**]. Here the water of life and of hope has become a torrential force of loss overwhelming her.

Other water images include the poisoned well Jane refers to on **page 203** [**198**], the rain that we find incorporated in many of the storm images, and, of course, the "stormy, scalding, heart-wrung tears" Jane sheds (**p.348**) [**361**].

h) Light.

There are many literal references to light - lamps and candles - in the novel, but they often take on, also, something of the same function as those of water - they suggest life and hope.

Lamps shine when Jane leaves Gateshead (**p.73**) [**51**], in the rooms and windows of Thornfield (repeatedly), and as a beacon when she approaches Moor House (**pp.357, 8**) [**371, 2**]. Light (good) is contrasted with darkness (evil), as when Jane brings a candle to shed light on the destruction which Bertha has wrought in Rochester's bedroom (**p.180**) [**169**].

It is also used metaphorically to mean understanding, perception, as when Helen Burns' "...powers woke, they kindled: first, they glowed in the bright tint of her cheek... then they shone in the liquid lustre of her eyes..." (**p.104**) [**85**], and when Jane tells St John, "'Nothing speaks or stirs in me while you talk. I am sensible of no light kindling - no life quickening... my mind is at this moment like a rayless dungeon'" (**p.428**) [**449**].

There are other kinds of light - we have already looked at moonlight; images of the sun and sunlight, or sunshine, are also found in the novel. On **page 294** [**298**] Rochester comments on Jane's mood, "'all the sunshine is gone'" and on **page 247** [**245**], with echoes of *Samson Agonistes* - as Margaret Smith points out - "'Still you are miserable; for hope has quitted you on the very confines of life: your sun at noon darkens in an eclipse'".

But there is also a contradictory use of light, as David Crompton indicates in his ***Jane Eyre*** *and the 'New Criticism'*: "...light represents conventional beauty of face and form and dark the reverse. Physically, Jane and Rochester (dark- haired, dark-eyed and plain) are opposed to the unsympathetic characters (many of whom are 'given' fair hair and blue or gray eyes)...", and he goes on to name Mrs Reed, St John Rivers, Blanche Ingram, amongst others. It would be unwise, then, to see light and dark polarised in too conventional a way in *Jane Eyre*. Their use is more complex than that.

i) **Dark.**

Darkness, like light, is used metaphorically in *Jane Eyre*. We first see its association with evil when Jane is sadistically locked in the red-room in the dark, and when Mr Lloyd, the apothecary, leaves the nursery, "...he closed the door after him, all the room darkened and my heart again sank" (**p.51**) [**27**].

On the night on which Bertha sets fire to Rochester's bed, Jane tells us, "I wished I had kept my candle burning: the night was drearily dark" (**p.178**) [**167**]. Her experiences have taught her to be afraid of the dark, not the literal dark of night, but the dark that is evil.

As light in *Jane Eyre* suggests life and hope, so darkness suggests the lack of these: when Jane fails to get a reply to her letter to Mrs Fairfax, "...my hope died out; and then I felt dark indeed" (**p.425**) [**445**]. Similarly, the path to Mr Rochester at Ferndean is gloomy, "The darkness of natural as well as of sylvan dusk, gathered over me..." (**p.455**) [**478**]. Both the setting of the house and the time of day - evening - as well as his blindness suggest the darkness in which he lives without Jane's love.

On the other hand, he is the dark Byronic hero, and it would be unwise to oversimplify these images of light and dark, as we said above.

j) *The Chestnut-tree.*

The chestnut-tree is a very powerful symbol in the novel. We are introduced to it first on **page 276** [**279**], as "a giant horse-chestnut, circled at the base by a seat", on which Jane and Rochester are going to sit on **page 280** [**282, 3**]. It is the place where he proposes to her and, just before he does so, "A waft of wind came sweeping down the laurel-walk, and trembled through the boughs of the chestnut: it wandered away - away - to an indefinite distance - it died" (**p.282**) [**285**]. After Rochester's declaration of love for Jane and his proposal, "I could scarcely see my master's face, near as I was. And what ailed the chestnut tree? it writhed and groaned; while wind roared in the laurel walk, and came sweeping over us" (**p.284**) [**287**]. The tree appears to become a symbol of their love, and the wind and storm which batter it and the lightning which strikes it (**p.285**) [**288**] represent the assaults on their love which are to follow.

Jane describes the lightning-struck tree on **page 304** [**309**]: "I faced the wreck of the chestnut tree; it stood up, black and riven: the trunk, split down the centre, gaped ghastly...The cloven halves were not broken from each other, for the firm base and strong roots kept them unsundered below; though community of vitality was destroyed - the sap could flow no more: their great boughs on each side were dead, and next winter's tempests would be sure to fell one or both to earth: as yet, however, they might be said to form one tree - a ruin; but an entire ruin". It is an ominous metaphorical description of what happens to or threatens Jane's and Rochester's love, though that love ultimately survives in a way the tree cannot.

At the end of the novel, on **page 469** [**493**], Rochester says to Jane, "'I am no better than the old, lightning-struck chestnut-tree in Thornfield orchard...And what right would that ruin have to bid a budding woodbine cover its decay with freshness?'" She replies - in a sustained natural metaphor - "'You are no ruin, sir - no lightning-struck tree: you are green and vigorous...'".

The tree, then, serves as a metaphor for what might have become of their love, given Rochester's unlawful proposal; and, indeed, for what appears to become of it after Mason's declaration in the church. It is an omen, but the ruin that it represents is avoided because of Jane's refusal to accept Rochester on his terms and his later redemption through self-sacrifice and suffering. The tree which Jane uses as a metaphor for him at the end of the novel is a living, 'bountiful', protective tree.

k) Birds.

The references to birds of all kinds are numerous in *Jane Eyre*. Many, of course, are literal, as the Arctic sea-fowl on **page 40** [**14**] and the rooks at Thornfield (**pp.131, 286, 448**) [**114,289,471**] - though it is possible to see a symbolic significance in these.

Many of the bird images are contained in similes: on **page 200** [**194**], Rochester's lady guests remind Jane of "a flock of white plumy birds" and later they "have become lively as larks", and one of them "chatters like a wren" (**p.205**) [**199**]. On **page 236** [**233**], Rochester ironically tells two of them to "return to your nests like a pair of doves, as you are".

Bird images are amongst Rochester's favourites for Jane. He likens her to "a wild, frantic bird" (**p.282**) [**284**], to "an eager bird" (**p.337**) [**349**], to a linnet on **page 339** [**351**]. She is his dove (**p.337**) [**348**] and his sky-lark (**p.464**) [**488**]. And on **pages 344** and **345** [**357**] there is a whole paragraph in which he talks of Jane in a sustained 'bird' metaphor. The images, of course, reflect the picture he has of her: an elusive, independent being from another world (she is also his 'elf' and his 'fairy'), but at the same time tender and gentle (dove).

He is a "fettered" bird and a "caged eagle" (**p.456**) [**479**]; his hair is "raven-black" and reminds Jane of "eagles' feathers", and "...whether your nails have grown like birds' claws or not, I have not yet noticed" (**p.461**) [**484,5**]. He is like "a royal eagle, chained to a perch" and she is "a sparrow" (**p.464**) [**488**]. Rochester, for Jane, is an eagle or a falcon, reflecting her idea of him as strong, powerful, noble. She sees him as 'caged' until set free by their love.

In addition to these, Jane describes her heart as "...impotent as a bird with both wings broken..." (**p.350**) [**364**]; Mason is a "sleek gander" compared with the "fierce falcon", Rochester, (**p.219**) [**215**] and Bertha is a "carrion-seeking bird of prey" (**p.240**) [**237**].

l) Animals.

As with birds, animal images abound in the novel. In the opening pages, John Reed calls Jane "bad animal ! " (**p .41**) [**15**], and she calls him, "Rat ! rat ! " (**p.43**) [**17**] . On **page 44** [**19**] Bessie says Jane is "like a mad cat" and on **page 59** [**36**] John Reed uses the same simile to describe her; on **page 58** [**34**] Miss Abbott calls her "little toad". All these images serve to dehumanize the characters they are describing, to rob them of their human worth and dignity.

Bertha is a "wild beast" and she makes a "snarling, canine noise" (**p.239**) [**237**]; Rochester refers to her room as "a wolf's-den" (**p.245**) [**243**] and a "wild beasts's den" (**p.336**) [**348**]. Jane, in contrast, is his "pet lamb" (**p.245**) [**243**], his "stray lamb" (**p.306**) [**312**], his "little ewe lamb" (**p.326**) [**336**]. He refers to himself as "toad", "ape" (**p.330**) [**341**] and "mole-eyed" (**p.333**) [**344**]. Once again, the images used of Bertha and of himself express the loathing he has for her and the self-disgust he feels at having married her. The image of the lamb that he uses when speaking of Jane is, of course, appealing and attractive and suggests her innocence and vulnerability.

There are many other animal references in the novel, used both literally and metaphorically: the "great black dog" of Bessie's stories (**p.52**) [**27**] and Pilot, "a lion-like creature" (**p.144**) [**128**]; the lizard on the crag and the bee on the bilberries at Whitcross (**p.351**) [**364**]; the "meek sheep", Mr Mason (**p.219**) [**215**], Jane, the "salamander" (**p.291**) [**294**] and Adèle, the "lap-dog" (**p.295**) [**299**].

m) Food.

We are made aware of food throughout the novel. On **page 53** [**28**] Bessie brings Jane a tart on a brightly painted china plate, but Jane is unable to eat it. At Lowood we are constantly reminded of food: the meagre rations, the burnt porridge, the feast of toast and seed-cake in Miss Temple's room; and the important place food has taken in Jane's imagination is emphasised when, her name finally cleared of all charges of dishonesty, she tells us, "...I forgot to prepare in imagination the Barmecide summer of hot roast potatoes, or white bread and new milk, with which I was wont to amuse my inward cravings: I feasted instead on the spectacle of ideal drawings..." (**p.106**) [**87**].

At Thornfield, where food is plentiful, we are told that she is greeted with "a little hot negus" and "a sandwich or two" (**p.127**) [**111**]; on **page 187** [**180**] tea is served in Mrs Fairfax's room, and we learn that Jane "ate so little at dinner"; and on **page 193** [**186**], Jane is drinking coffee, while Adèle has another bun and another mug of milk. While Rochester's guests are dressing for dinner, we hear what is being cooked in the kitchen, and that Jane "...took possession of a cold chicken, a roll of bread, some tarts, a plate or two and a knife and fork" (**p.197**) [**190**] for her and Adèle's supper.

On her leaving Thornfield, she is faced again with privation and want, and the craving for food is expressed, particularly, as she wanders from Whitcross to Morton and Moor House. She asks the woman in a bread shop to let her have a roll in exchange for her handkerchief or gloves; she begs a piece of bread from a farmer and a "mess of cold porridge" from a girl about to feed it to pigs (**pp.354-356**) [**368,9**]. And at Moor House she has to be restrained from eating too much too quickly (**p.363**) [**377**].

As we look at the pattern of these images, it is tempting to see these many references to food as metaphors for Jane's emotional needs. Certainly, they are literal references, too; but Charlotte Brontë's persistent preoccupation with food in all its detail does suggest a more-than-literal intention.

When Jane is settled at Lowood and at Moor House, the references to lack of or poor food either cease altogether or become much fewer; in metaphorical terms, she is being sufficiently emotionally nourished. And the plentiful supply of food at Thornfield suggests her emotional nourishment there is satisfying and fulfilling.

Food is sometimes used in a more obviously metaphorical sense in the novel: On **pages 387** and **388** [**404**], St John tells Jane that we sometimes have to "...turn the bent of nature...and when our energies seem to demand a *sustenance* they cannot get...we need neither *starve* from inanition, nor stand still in despair: we have but to seek another *nourishment* for the mind, as strong as the forbidden *food* it longed to taste...", and when Jane hears that she is their uncle's heir, "I again felt rather like an individual of but average *gastronomical* powers, sitting down to *feast* alone at a table spread with *provisions* for a hundred" (**p.409**) [**427**].

n) Paradise/Eden.

The words 'Paradise', 'Eden', 'elysium' are used on several occasions in *Jane Eyre*, not without irony on some of them.

We are told, on **page 276** [**278**], that the orchard where Rochester proposes to Jane is sheltered and "Eden-like" and, when he has told her of his love, she thinks of being "...called to the paradise of union..." (**p.284**) [**287**]. In view of what awaits them, the terms are certainly ironical here. Later, when speaking to St John, she is to refer to Thornfield as "a house I had found a paradise" (**p.374**) [**389**], and on **page 379** [**394**] she reflects on her "...racking regrets for my broken idol and lost elysium...".

Rochester, too, speaks of the "...green flowery Eden..." in Jane's brain (**p.340**) [**352**]; and Jane - talking of St John's love for Rosamond Oliver - says he would not "...relinquish, for the elysium of her love, one hope of the true, eternal Paradise" (**p.394**) [**411**].

Taken together, all these references suggest an ironical mocking of the belief in an earthly paradise or Eden - at least, in the simple terms in which Jane sees it in the orchard. She is to come to rest with Rochester in some sort of Eden, but it is hard-won and grounded in reality and truth. St John, we feel, is right to reject an elysium with Rosamond - it would have been no such thing!

Notes:

STRUCTURE (Q.20).

The structure of *Jane Eyre* is dictated by the kind of novel it is - what Barbara Hardy calls "...an education novel, showing the growth from childhood to maturity, tracing a development in moral insight and conduct".

Jane's growth from childhood to maturity is structured around certain places: her life as a small child at Gateshead, her schooling and growing to young adulthood at Lowood, her life as a governess and falling in love at Thornfield, her discovery of a 'family' to which she belongs and her rejection of a loveless marriage at Moor House, her return to Rochester and a happy and fulfilling marriage at Ferndean.

The 'plot' of the novel is the development of the main character, who learns - through education, self-discipline and determination - to reconcile the conflict in her own character between nature and principle, between imagination and reason. The growth is progressive: the lessons learnt earlier stengthen Jane for each successive fight.

There are, of course, setbacks in this moral progression, or she would not be human, nor a credible heroine. Jane herself recognises the most important of these lapses when she tells us at the end of Chapter 24, "My future husband was becoming to me my whole world: almost my hope of heaven. He stood between me and every thought of religion, as an eclipse intervenes between man and the broad sun. I could not, in those days, see God for his creature: of whom I had made an idol" (**p.302**) [**307**]. Rochester enjoys a place in her heart and mind which only God should occupy - she will pay dearly for this lapse, as Rochester must pay for his attempt to flout the law of both Church and state. As we have already seen, though, they do pay through suffering and self-sacrifice and are rewarded with lasting happiness together.

Notes:

ASPECTS OF STYLE (Q.21).

We have already looked at various aspects of Charlotte Brontë's style in *Jane Eyre*, particularly her extensive use of imagery, including metaphor and simile. We are going to look now briefly at a few of the other devices which proliferate in the novel: the use of antithesis, personification, rhetorical questions; the repeated use of the imperative 'Reader', St John's rhetoric and Helen Burns' language.

a) ***Antithesis:*** The use of antithesis contributes to the balanced rhythm of Charlotte Brontë's prose. On **page 431** [**452**], St John tells Jane, "I want a wife: the sole helpmeet I can influence efficiently in life, and retain absolutely till death." The rhetorical ring of the words 'life' and 'death' strike a chill into the heart of Jane, claiming as they do complete ownership of, and power over, her.

It is interesting to note how many of the examples of antithesis are either used by St John or in connection with him. They are a powerful aspect of his rhetorical language: "I am the servant of an infallible master", he tells Jane on **page 427** [**447**], and she, on **page 443** [**465**] - influenced by his persuasive words and manner - says, "The Impossible - i.e. my marriage with St John - was fast becoming the Possible". On **page 446** [**468**] she speaks of her spirit - already juxtaposed with her flesh - being strong enough "... to grope an outlet from this cloud of doubt, and find the open day of certainty". Here, the antithesis emphasises the struggle she is having to overcome doubt with certainty.

b) ***Personification:*** The personification of abstract nouns serves to emphasise their importance - make them come alive for the reader as real forces. When Rochester - disguised as the old gipsy woman - is telling Jane's fortune, he says he can read in her forehead that, "'Reason sits firm and holds the reins, and she will not let the feelings burst away and hurry her to wild chasms. The passions may rage furiously, like true heathens, as they are; and the desires may imagine all sorts of vain things: but judgement shall still have the last word in every argument, and the casting vote in every decision" (**p.230**) [**227**]. Reason will have the upper hand when the moment of crisis comes - he forecasts truly from his understanding of her conflict between nature and principle - and the personification here presents reason, passions and desires as the forceful combatants in the struggle.

We have already seen how Hope is personified on **page 107** [**88**] when spring comes to Lowood, emphasising Jane's new mood as she enjoys the new life that spring brings, not only in the natural world which she is enjoying, but in the new-found liberty and better food that have been introduced as a result of the typhus epidemic at the school.

Again, we find personification on **page 190** [**182,3**], where Jane is reasoning with herself when she finds Rochester has left Thornfield without telling her: "Arraigned at my own bar, Memory having given her evidence of the hopes, wishes, sentiments I had been cherishing since last night - of the general state of mind in which I had indulged for nearly a fortnight past; Reason having come forward and told, in her own quiet way, a plain, unvarnished tale, showing how I had rejected the real and rabidly devoured the ideal; - I pronounced judgement to this effect..." and the judgement that she pronounces on herself is that "...a greater fool than Jane Eyre had never breathed the breath of life..."

This last example, presenting Memory and Reason as defendant and witness or prosecutor in a court of law, effectively reinforces the conflict between nature and principle once again. She forces herself to discipline her feelings, her imagination with reason and judgement. The use of personification highlights the struggle that dominates the novel.

c) ***Rhetorical questions:*** These raise questions which do not really require an answer. They ask what the narrator wants to draw attention to, or sometimes what we, the readers, are thinking or should be thinking. They are there for effect; the use of them is a way of creating suspense or interest. On **page 79** [**57**], for instance, when the whole school rises, Jane, the narrator, asks, "What was the matter?", drawing our attention to the entry of Miss Temple which interrupts Jane's observations.

When Jane tells us that she spends much time with a girl called Ann Wilson, we are wondering what her rhetorical questions ask, "And where, meantime, was Helen Burns? Why did I not spend these sweet days of liberty with her? Had I forgotten her; or was I so worthless as to have grown tired of her pure society?" (**p.109**) [**91**]. The questions afford Jane - who knows the answers - an effective opportunity to remind us of Helen and her worth.

On **page 271** [**274**] Jane makes a comment about her own passionate desires when she asks "But what is so headstrong as youth? What so blind as inexperience?" And she draws dramatic attention to St. John's manner when she asks, on **page 437** [**459**], "Reader, do you know, as I do, what terror those cold people can put into the ice of their questions? How much of the fall of the avalanche is in their anger? of the breaking up of the frozen sea in their displeasure?"

d) ***Reader:*** This is a device - sometimes a rather irritating one - by which the writer draws the reader's attention to what she is saying or invites the reader to share her point of view or remember something she has said before. Often, it is in the vocative, as on **pages 109, 125, 214, 354-355, 449** [**91,108,210,368-9,471**] and, best known of all, on **page 474** [**498**], at the beginning of the last chapter, where she tells us "Reader, I married him".

On other occasions she uses not the vocative, but the third person, as on pages **80** [**57**], "Let the reader add...", **204** [**198**], "...the reader knows..." and on **pages 439** [**460**] and **444** [**466**].

e)   ***St John's rhetoric:*** We have already mentioned the rhetorical use of antithesis in St. John's language. There are other rhetorical devices we should look at here. Notice the emotional and cumulative effect of "...my king, my lawgiver, my captain, is the All-perfect", as he describes God to Jane on **page 427** [**447**], and he goes on to say "It seems strange to me that all round me do not burn to enlist under the same banner". The use of the word 'burn' and the vision of God as captain, surrounded by a mighty army, are there for dramatic effect: they are used to persuade Jane to join him. Jane says, rather ironically, on **page 430** [**450**], "He prizes me as a soldier would a good weapon".

On **page 429** [**449**], he says of Jane, "I recognised a soul that revelled in the flame and excitement of sacrifice", again an attempt to persuade her through emotive imagery. His is the language of the preacher, the man obsessed with a cause, the missionary he is to become. It has a biblical ring to it, an echo of many of the famous and stirring hymns of the nineteenth century. Ironically, despite his passionate language, St John is a cold man towards his fellow human-beings.

f)   ***Helen Burns' language:*** In contrast to St John's, Helen's language is rational, calm, impersonal, while reflecting in its imagery as firm a belief in God and in eternity as St John professes. On **page 91** [**70**] she cautions Jane to control her "passionate emotions" and says of herself, "'I live in calm, looking to the end'". Young as she is, she has learnt the self-discipline and objectivity that enable her to bear suffering and humiliation with the patience of a saint.

There is nothing in the decription of Helen that suggests she is lacking the human qualities which St John is without. Jane tells us of Helen, "...her spirit seemed hastening to live within a very brief span as much as many live during a protracted existence" (**p.105**) [**85**]. Both she and St John have their sights firmly on another world, but how different they are as characters!

There are many aspects of style we could have looked at; these are just a few of them.

Notes:

THE ROLE OF THE NARRATOR (Q.22).

Jane, of course, is both narrator and heroine of the novel. She tells her own story and she does so through narrative and dialogue, reminding us often that this is a story, with her "Reader! - I forgave him at the moment, and on the spot" (**p.326**) [**336**] and "Gentle reader, may you never feel what I then felt!" (**p.348**) [**361**].

She tells her story looking back on the past, though we are aware of this only at rare moments in such phrases as "what I then felt" (above) and "in those days" at the end of Chapter 24. For us to be aware of this all the time would be to lose the sense of suspense and dramatic conflict which is necessary if we are to maintain interest and involvement in Jane's story. And there is considerable suspense, centred particularly on Grace Poole/Bertha and on Rochester's relationship with Blanche Ingram, though Jane's wandering before she finds Moor House and the revelation of her identity there - hinted at in St John's actions and attitude - also contribute to the suspense.

The suspense created around Rochester's relationship with Blanche Ingram lasts for a considerable portion of the novel, and it is worth noting here that Rochester's behaviour during this period is not only unkind to Blanche, for whom we have no sympathy, but it is positively sadistic in places to Jane. He tells her "... I have already, through my future-mother-in-law, heard of a place that I think will suit" (**p.279**) [**282**] and he allows her to be reduced to sobbing "convulsively" (**p.280**) [**283**] - all this just moments before he tells her he loves her and proposes to her. Rochester, here, unattractively joins the other sadistic characters in the novel, notably Mrs Reed and Mr Brocklehurst. Jane, then, as narrator, though she doesn't pass comment on this behaviour, does record it honestly: she presents him with all the faults for which he has to do penance if he is to deserve her at the end.

One of the devices the narrator employs is irony. Robert Heilman, in his Charlotte Brontë's 'New' Gothic in **Jane Eyre** and **Villette**, suggests an ironical modification of the traditional Gothic in *Jane Eyre* which is worth looking at: he gives as one of the examples of this Charlotte's ironical apology to the "'romantic reader' for telling 'the plain truth' that Grace generally bears a 'pot of porter'". By using irony in her use of the Gothic, then, Jane is introducing a moderating, realistic element to the traditionally romantic device.

We have already noted the irony at the beginning of Chapter 9, when new life and hope come to Lowood with the spring - that is not all the new season brings: typhus sweeps through the school and Helen Burns dies of consumption.

Romantic illusion and hope are soon counteracted or modified by reality.

If *Jane Eyre* is a novel about the conflict between nature and principle, passion and reason, then the narrator must express that conflict in the way she presents her story - to modify the romantic ironically is one of the ways in which she achieves this.

Notes:

HOSTILITY TO *JANE EYRE* ON PUBLICATION (Q.23).

On the whole, *Jane Eyre* was very well received, becoming an immediate success and running into three editions within a few months of being published in October 1847.

There were, however, some critical voices, and we're going to look at their main objections to the novel here. They fall into three main categories:

a) Improbability - of plot, incident and character;

b) Coarseness;

c) Its questionable moral and religious tone/attitude.

There were other criticisms besides these: the author's failure to create a sympathetic hero or heroine, Charlotte Brontë's lack of knowledge about fashionable clothing and the behaviour of ladies of the upper classes, that the 'dénouement' is "too abrupt" and incidents "too crowded", that there is too much "artifice" in the novel. You can find all of these explained, elaborated on and illustrated in the reviews at the beginning of the Casebook on *Jane Eyre* and *Villette*.

a) Improbability:

This is by far the most common criticism of *Jane Eyre* in early reviews. H.F. Chorley in *Athenaeum*, 23 October 1847 complains that, after the revelation of Rochester's marriage, "the heroine [is] too outrageously tried, and too romantically assisted in her difficulties: - until arrives the last moment, at which obstacles fall down like the battlements of 'Castle Melodrame'..." He is criticising here, presumably, Jane's wandering hungry and begging around Morton, the unlikely stumbling upon her own cousins and a fortune, perhaps the pressure that St John puts upon her to marry him, and the final revelation that Rochester is free to marry her, after the 'supernatural' call that summons her to him.

Another critic says of the novel: "...its truth is not probable in the principal incidents, and still less in the manner in which the characters influence the incidents so as to produce conduct". (*The Spectator*, 6 November 1847).

And G.H. Lewes, who describes it as "a book after our own heart", cannot help seeing "...some defects in it - defects which the excellence of the rest only brings into stronger relief. There is, indeed, too much melodrama and improbability, which smack of the circulating-library - we allude particularly to the mad wife and all that relates to her, and to the wanderings of Jane when she quits Thornfield; yet even those parts are powerfully executed" (*Fraser's Magazine*, December 1847).

And a reviewer in *Christian Remembrancer*, April 1848, writes, " The plot is most extravagantly improbable, verging all along upon the supernatural, and at last running fairly into it. All the power is shown and all the interest lies in the characters..." In spite of this last comment, he goes on to write of the improbable nature of Helen Burns: She "...is meant to be a perfect Christian, and is a simple seraph..."

In October 1848 a reviewer in *Revue des Deux Mondes*, Eugène Forçade, added his voice on the subject: "...the plot here is the weak side of the work. I cannot understand why the author of *Jane Eyre* could not have found a simpler action through which to develop her situation and characters; I cannot understand why she should have thought she needed to have such complicated and disjointed incidents, often improbably linked". The review in general was extremely positive and Charlotte herself was delighted with it, commenting, "...The censures are as well-founded as the commendations".

The last of our examples in this section are taken from a very hostile review by Elizabeth Rigby, published in *Quarterly Review*, December 1848. In it she writes that the hero and heroine "...do things which, though not impossible, lie utterly beyond the bounds of probability", and she later refers to it as a tale in which "...the reader may trace gross inconsistencies and improbabilities".

b) Coarseness:

Elizabeth Rigby has much to say on this subject, claiming that "...it is stamped with a coarseness of language and laxity of tone" and is marked by "...sheer rudeness and vulgarity". She refers later to Jane's "gross vulgarity". And, speculating on the authorship of the novel, she writes, "...Whoever it be, it is a person who, with great mental powers, combines a total ignorance of the habits of society, a great coarseness of taste, and a heathenish doctrine of religion..."

The reviewer in *The Spectator*, 6 November 1847, quoted above, also talks of the "low tone of behaviour (rather than of morality) in the book".

The editor of the Casebook, Miriam Allott, has a very useful and interesting section in her Introduction on what reviewers meant by 'Coarseness': to one it was "the provincial setting, speech and behaviour of Charlotte's Yorkshire characters", for others it "...referred to the indecorous presentation of her characters' love affairs, which were conducted in an unusually outspoken manner and in unconventional settings". To others, it "...had to do with the sardonic handling of such 'upper classs' characters as Blanche Ingram and her mother..." and to others it "...was associated with the manner in which she dealt with Church matters and religion..."

c) Its questionable moral and religious tone/attitude:

The reviewer in *Christian Remembrancer*, April 1848, comments, "To say that *Jane Eyre* is positively immoral or antichristian, would be to do its writer an injustice. Still it wears a questionable aspect...The authoress of *Jane Eyre* will have power in her generation, whether she chooses to exercise it for good or evil..."

Elizabeth Rigby has no such qualms as the previous writer shows. In her opinion, "...the autobiography of Jane Eyre is pre-eminently an anti-Christian composition. There is throughout it a murmuring against the comforts of the rich and the privations of the poor, which, as far as each individual is concerned, is a murmuring against God's appointment..." We are reminded of the verse of the hymn "All things bright and beautiful", which we no longer sing, being perhaps not quite so ready to attribute to "God's appointment" the injustices and inequalites of society:

> "The rich man in his castle,
> The poor man at his gate,
> God made them, high and lowly,
> And order'd their estate."

Elizabeth Rigby has this to say about Jane herself: "It is true Jane does right, and exerts great moral strength, but it is the strength of a mere heathen mind which is a law unto itself. No Christian grace is perceptible upon her. She has inherited in fullest measure the worst sin of our fallen nature - the sin of pride..."

Elsewhere, the same writer declares that the author of *Jane Eyre*, has committed the "...highest moral offence a novel writer can commit, that of making an unworthy character interesing in the eyes of the reader. Mr Rochester is a man who deliberately and secretly seeks to violate the laws both of God and man, and yet we will be bound half our lady readers are enchanted with him for a model of generosity and honour. We would have thought that such a hero had had no chance, in the purer taste of the present day; but the popularity of *Jane Eyre* is a proof how deeply the love of the illegimate romance is implanted in our nature..."

It would be a pity to leave *Jane Eyre* on this critical note. The vast majority of the reviews, as we have said, were full of admiration for and curiosity about who this "Currer Bell" could be. Thackeray wrote in a letter to W.S. Williams, who had sent him a copy of the novel, "...I have been exceedingly moved and pleased by *Jane Eyre*. It is a woman's writing, but whose? Give my respects and thanks to the author, whose novel is the first English one (and the French are only romances now) that I've been able to read for many a day..." And G.H. Lewes wrote in his review of December 1847, "...man or woman, young or old, be that as it may, no such book has gladdened our eyes for a long while. Almost all that we require in a novelist she has: perception of character, and power of delineating it; picturesqueness; passion; and knowledge of life. The story is not only of singular interest, naturally evolved, unflagging to the last, but it fastens itself upon your attention, and will not leave you. The book closed, the enchantment continues..."

Notes:

SELECT BIBLIOGRAPHY

Alexander, Christine
and Jane Sellars
The Art of the Brontës, Cambridge
University Press, 1995

Allott, Miriam, ed.
*Charlotte Brontë: **Jane Eyre** and **Villette***,
Casebook Series, Macmillan Education, 1987

Berman, Ronald
Charlotte Brontë's Natural History, Brontë
Society 'Transactions', Vol.18, No.4, 1984

Chard, M J
*Apple of Discord: Centrality of the Eden Myth in
Charlotte Brontë's Novels*, Brontë Society
'Transactions', Vol. 19, Part 5, 1988

Fraser, Rebecca
Charlotte Brontë, Methuen, London, 1988

Gaskell, Elizabeth
The Life of Charlotte Brontë, Smith, Elder
& Co., 1873

Gerin, W
Charlotte Brontë, The Evolution of Genius, Oxford
University Press, 1971

Hardy, Barbara
Jane Eyre, Basil Blackwell, 1964

Lloyd Evans, B & G
Everyman's Companion to the Brontës, J M Dent
& Sons Ltd., 1982

Loe, Thomas
*Rejection and Progress in **Jane Eyre***, Brontë
Society 'Transactions', Vol. 19, Part 8, 1989

O'Neill, Judith, ed.
Critics on Charlotte and Emily Brontë, George
Allen and Unwin Ltd., 1977

Sellars, Jane
*Art and the Artist as Heroine in the Novels of
Charlotte, Emily and Anne Brontë*, Brontë Society
'Transactions', Vol.20, Part 2, 1990

Spark, Muriel, ed.
The Brontë Letters, Macmillan, 1966